BLUEPRINTS

Writing

Jim Fitzsimmons

Rhona Whiteford

Stanley Thornes (Publishers) Ltd

Do you receive BLUEPRINTS NEWS?

Blueprints is an expanding series of practical teacher's ideas books and photocopiable resources for use in primary schools. Books are available for separate infant and junior age ranges for every core and foundation subject, as well as for an ever widening range of other primary teaching needs. These include **Blueprints Primary English** books and **Blueprints Resource Banks**. **Blueprints** are carefully structured around the demands of the National Curriculum in England and Wales, but are used successfully by schools and teachers in Scotland, Northern Ireland and elsewhere.

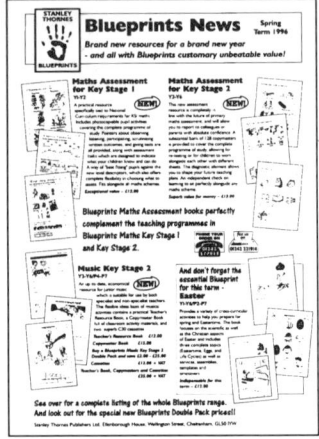

Blueprints provide:
- *Total curriculum coverage*
- *Hundreds of practical ideas*
- *Books specifically for the age range you teach*
- *Flexible resources for the whole school or for individual teachers*
- *Excellent photocopiable sheets – ideal for assessment and children's work profiles*
- *Supreme value.*

Books may be bought by credit card over the telephone and information obtained on **(01242) 577944**. Alternatively, photocopy and return this **FREEPOST** form to receive **Blueprints News**, our regular update on all new and existing titles. You may also like to add the name of a friend who would be interested in being on the mailing list.

Please add my name to the **BLUEPRINTS NEWS** mailing list.

Mr/Mrs/Miss/Ms _____

Home address _____

_____ Postcode _____

School address _____

_____ Postcode _____

Please also send **BLUEPRINTS NEWS** to:

Mr/Mrs/Miss/Ms _____

Address _____

_____ Postcode _____

To: Marketing Services Dept., Stanley Thornes Ltd, FREEPOST (GR 782), Cheltenham, GL50 1BR

© Text Jim Fitzsimmons and Rhona Whiteford 1989
© Illustrations ST(P) Ltd 1989

Illustrations by Rhona Whiteford

First published in 1989

First published in new binding in 1998 by:
Stanley Thornes (Publishers) Ltd
Ellenborough House
Wellington Street
CHELTENHAM GL50 1YW
England

98 99 00 01 02 / 10 9 8 7 6 5 4 3 2 1

Typeset by Tech-Set, Gateshead, Tyne & Wear
Printed and bound in Great Britain by
Redwood Books, Trowbridge, Wiltshire

British Library Cataloguing in Publication Data

Fitzsimmons, Jim
    Blueprints Writing
    1. Great Britain. Primary schools.
    Curriculum subjects: Writing skills. Teaching aids
    I. Title   II. Whiteford, Rhona
    372.6'23

ISBN 0–7487–3467–8

CONTENTS

TOPIC INDEX

These headings are common primary school topics. They are followed by numbers of the photocopiable sheets in this book which would be useful for each topic.

Ourselves   1–10, 12–14, 21, 40

Feelings   1, 8, 11, 12, 14, 21, 40, 41, 53

Animals   13, 24, 27–30, 35, 37, 47, 58

Pets   2, 7, 13, 23, 35, 54

Nature/Environment   10, 16–20, 27–30, 35, 55, 58

Neighbourhood   3–6, 8–10, 35–7, 61, 62, 68, 69

Space   42–45

Time   21–30, 40, 61, 62, 64, 66–8

Air   20, 43, 50

Water   16–20, 27–30, 39, 51, 52, 58

Changes   2, 4, 5, 14, 15, 21, 27–30, 40, 44, 45, 49, 50, 55, 60

Weather   11, 16–20, 27–30

Spring   10, 11, 16, 20, 27, 35

Summer   10, 11, 16, 19, 28, 35, 36, 58

Autumn   10, 11, 16, 18, 20, 22, 23, 29, 35

Winter   10, 11, 16–18, 20, 24–6, 30

Homes   3, 5, 8, 24, 31–4, 37, 46, 49, 51, 55

Food   1, 9, 11, 13, 19, 21, 25–30, 33, 37, 60, 70

Clothes   1, 7, 11, 15–17, 19, 25, 26, 31, 39, 40, 44–6, 56, 57

Transport   9, 10, 42–6, 50, 51, 54, 61, 62

Entertainment   10, 12, 13, 15, 17, 19, 21–3, 25–37, 42, 50, 56–60

Holidays   2, 7, 10, 16, 19, 27–30, 35–7, 40, 42, 43, 49–51, 55–8, 61, 62

Communications   12, 42–5, 49, 59, 60, 63–70

Fantasy   7, 13, 15, 25, 26, 31–4, 38, 41–52, 54, 55, 60, 69

The Past   1–5, 7, 8, 10, 42, 50, 51, 55, 60, 63–6, 68

INTRODUCTION

Blueprints: Writing provides a varied and extensive resource for developing many different kinds of writing with infants and lower juniors. It consists of 71 photocopiable writing sheets, photocopiable topic word lists and story starters/endings, and suggestions for using the photocopiable sheets in class.

The sheets do not aim to provide a definitive progression of skills and experiences, but rather to be a flexible resource: each sheet can be used in many ways as part of your own writing strategy. In the section *Using the sheets* we have included ideas on their use for stories, descriptions, letters, posters, cards, poems, news sheets, recipes, word lists, charts and many other types of written language. Developing a sense of writing for different audiences and purposes is an important feature of the book. *Using the sheets* also gives suggestions for incorporating the finished writing into classroom displays. In addition, many of the sheets can be used as a resource for topic work. The topic index on page iv cross-references the sheets in this way.

All the sheets can be used with top infants and lower juniors. However, you will find the first third of the book most appropriate for reception children, as the sheets have been chosen to be developmentally appropriate for younger age groups. Subsequent sheets begin to provide opportunities for more extensive use of the imagination, as older infants develop this facility and greater language versatility.

Your own teaching strategy will play a part in the motivation to write but we think that children and teachers respond to variety and novelty wisely used. The ideas in this book will stimulate the children's imaginations and encourage them to produce exciting and varied responses.

The sheets can be used with individuals, small groups or the whole class, but it is, of course, essential to provide stimulus and to do some preparatory work before the children start. Discussion is vital to language development and allows for interchange of ideas on vocabulary, approach and content. Initial stimulus might also come from outside sources: a school trip, an item brought in from home, a visitor to the school, a painting, a piece of music or a TV programme. Most of the sheets can be used as resources for this kind of stimulus, and we give many stimulus ideas for individual sheets in the next section. You may, however, find some of the following practical suggestions valuable in getting the most out of *Blueprints: Writing*.

Try-out sheets

The idea of drafting is an important one to develop with children. As part of your writing strategy why not photocopy two sheets per child and use one for the child to keep for rough work – trying out spellings and ideas – and the other for the finished product. Nobody gets everything right first time!

Make a class vocabulary sheet

If you can, enlarge the sheet you want to use to A3 size and write on it the words that the children suggest. Pin this up for class use when writing. You may, of course, need to use two or three such sheets. Alternatively, draw the outline of the sheet on the blackboard and use in a similar way.

Add a topic section to children's own dictionaries

Photocopy the vocabulary sheets in this book and give a copy of each strip to each child to stick in his/her own dictionary, in a topic section, perhaps at the back of the book. Do one page a week as a reading exercise for older children or add the sheet as you do a particular topic.

Make a topic vocabulary book

Photocopy pages that illustrate particular topics – the seasons, our class, the park, the zoo, etc. – and staple them together as a book with a paper cover. Add vocabulary to each page, either weekly or as you go on a trip or do a topic or an assembly on the subject. You could reduce the size of your photocopy sheet to A5, which would save on paper and space and make it a more manageable reference booklet for use at cramped tables.

Using the vocabulary sheets

These sheets can be photocopied and cut up so that each child has his/her own list at the start of the appropriate topic. After your initial stimulus, you will probably want to spend some time discussing words which might be needed for written work. These lists provide the most common words used for the topics, and it would be useful if the children could stick them in the back of their personal dictionaries for continued reference.

Make your own copymaster

The sheets can be used as the framework for your own language activities. Photocopy a sheet, then add your own vocabulary list or language exercise – a cloze procedure or prediction exercise, for example – with a fine black pen. Then photocopy your personalised sheet for use by the children.

Make books from the sheets

Photocopy several sheets for each child (if they write long stories!) so that they can continue the story on similarly decorated pages. Staple the sheets together as a book and put a paper cover on it. Children can colour in the design on each page or leave it black and white, and draw their own cover picture. If you can reduce the pages, you could make small A5 books which children sometimes like.

Make big books

If you can enlarge your photocopies to A3, the sheets can be used as a focus for class writing or to make big books.

Make zig-zag books

Use several repeat sheets to write a story or gather written information. Then mount these on paper and concertina it. You may want to reduce the sheet size to A5; or keep the size to A4 or even A3 to make a class book for table top or wall display.

Make shaped books

Using one of the large-shape sheets in this book, such as the clown or the snowman, cut out round however many pages have been used for the story or for other writing and staple them together at the left side. Use one sheet as a cover and decorate it.

Use reduced sheets for special purposes

Reduce the sheet to A5 to allow it to fit into exercise books or to make greetings cards, or indeed for the reluctant writer! You may also need a smaller sheet for poems and verses.

Enlarge sheets for displays

Enlarge the sheet to A3 and use as a title sheet or illustration on your display, e.g. the teddy bear, the alien, the clown.

Use a drawing to stimulate writing

Some of the sheets have a scene with a space in the middle or at the bottom. If you photocopy two sheets you can use one as an initial ideas sheet by asking the children to draw or note down what they think will be in the space. This will give them the chance to stretch their imaginations and get their minds 'in gear' for the writing. For some of the sheets this would be a good idea for the initial stimulus.

Ways to start and end a story: How to use the sheets

Once children have passed the stage of needing the security of a well-known and learned start to their writing (such as 'One day I . . .', or 'Here is a . . .'), they can be presented with different formulae which will widen their horizons and increase confidence. If given in an accessible form, the frustration sometimes associated with actually putting pen to paper may be prevented. Children will soon memorise the selection of phrases even if they cannot read every word and familiarity will broaden reading experience. The children should be encouraged to use a different beginning and ending for each story, having first discussed the story theme and decided if the phrases are appropriate to the story contents. This will help them to write and to read for meaning and will form a valuable part of your language teaching.

The sheets can be reproduced in different ways: they can be photocopied on A5 paper for individual use and could be stuck in the back of the writing book or personal dictionary. If A5 paper is not available, make two copies from the mastersheet at A5 size, trim these to fit side by side on the copier to fill the A4 grid, then reproduce what you need.

The sheets can also be copied on A3 paper to make a wall chart for class reference. Colour in the illustrations and mount on appropriate coloured backing paper. A4 copies can be stuck on the wall, on cupboards or on workcards for group reference.

Double sheets

You will see that some activities are spread over two sheets, e.g. the clown and the train. The first sheet can be used on its own or the second can be introduced as a supplementary sheet and for displays. Indeed, the train can be as long as the child can write!

Titles

We have put a title and sheet number on each sheet for easy reference but you can replace the title with one of your own or one suggested by the children. Cover the printed title with paper before you photocopy. There is also room on each sheet for you to decide where you want children to put their names and the date.

1   ALL ABOUT ME ▶

Starting point

Discuss the children's appearance, likes and dislikes. Get the children to bring in photos of themselves as babies or toddlers, and come in to school wearing their favourite clothes. They could also bring in a favourite toy.

Ask the chldren to describe themselves, e.g. 'I am five. My name is Ben. I have blond hair. I like school and I like cars', etc. Two sheets are given: one for boys and one for girls.

Other writing ideas

The children could write on their sheets about various things, e.g. *When I was small*; *Growing up*; *My little brother/sister*. Use the sheet also as a personal vocabulary record.

Display ideas

Before doing their writing, the children colour the figures to represent themselves. These can then be cut out to make hanging displays, or you could make a giant zig-zag book by taping together six of the children's sheets.

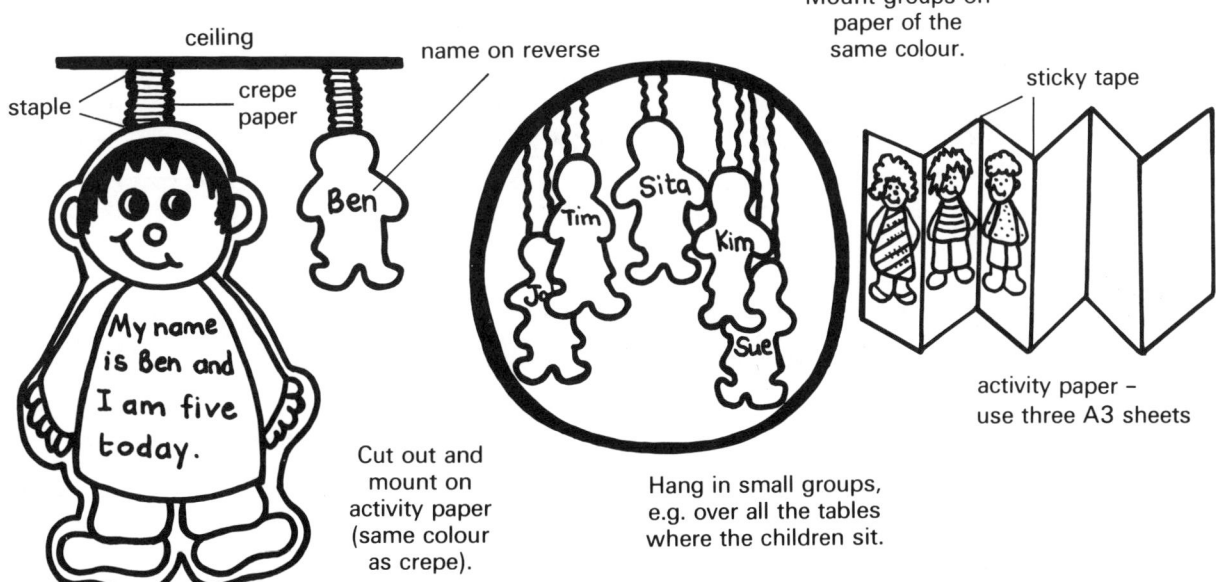

ceiling

staple

crepe paper

name on reverse

My name is Ben and I am five today.

Ben

Cut out and mount on activity paper (same colour as crepe).

Tim · Sita · Kim · Jo · Sue

Hang in small groups, e.g. over all the tables where the children sit.

Mount groups on paper of the same colour.

sticky tape

activity paper – use three A3 sheets

2   MY FAMILY ▶

Starting point

The children could bring in photos of their family or make a family using toys from the home corner. Discuss family activities and habits, e.g. 'We all go swimming on Sundays'. Discuss the people in the family, who they are, what jobs they do, why the child loves them, etc.

The children write their own family stories on the sheet. If there is more than one child in the family, the writer can add other drawings. Be sensitive to different family situations. For example, if your class includes children from one-parent families, give all the children the choice of using either this sheet or sheet 3 *My house*. Then they can write about who lives in the house.

Other writing ideas

The children could write other stories about *The new neighbours* or *The funny family* (aliens, monsters, clowns, etc.). To provide stimulus, let the children bring in fantasy toys and look at pictures. A visit to a circus, if possible, would provide a wealth of ideas.

Starting point

Arrange a walk outside school to look at different types of houses. Discuss what you have seen and allow the children to describe their own home and bedroom. Each child can then write a description of his or her own home.

Other writing ideas

The sheet can be used for story writing – *Goldilocks and the Three Bears; Hansel and Gretel; The inventor's house; Haunted house; House of the future.* The children can adapt the basic illustration to suit their titles. Animal homes make popular subjects for factual writing.

    To stimulate interest, the children could bring in toy homes, e.g. dolls' houses, castles, fantasy kingdoms, or pictures of these. Arrange a trip to a local nature reserve or watch video extracts from nature programmes to see different animal homes. As part of your art and craft work, make a large picture of *The witch's house.*

Display ideas

Make a book, using the house picture as the cover.

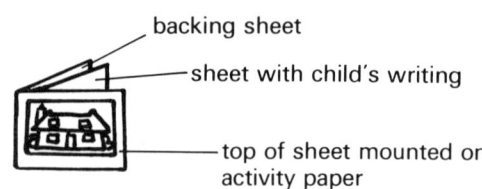

- backing sheet
- sheet with child's writing
- top of sheet mounted on activity paper

Make a frieze of a scene similar to your school neighbourhood.

Make a background scene with activity paper of different colours.

Staple little books to the scene, as houses.

white for clouds

pale blue

shades of green for bushes

brown

children's drawings of cars, cut out

yellow

We have all written about our own house.

Starting point

Discuss memories of the first day: How did the children feel? Were they frightened, lonely, excited? Was it a friendly or a strange place? The children can then write about their own memories.

Other writing ideas

Possible subjects are *Space school; Dancing school; Karate class; Gymnastics class.* Ask the children to bring in the outfits they wear for their sports and get them to try and recall what is was like when they started, and to say what skills they have acquired.

Display idea

Mount a display of sports equipment used in school.

Starting point

Discuss class activities, the people who help in class, the friends the children like to work with. Make a large wall picture like a class 'photo' using each child's self-portrait (sheet 1 could be used for these). Involve maths by drawing graphs of the number of boys/girls, hair colour, eye colour, height.

Other writing ideas

The children would enjoy writing about *A rather strange class* or *When grown-ups came to school.* Discuss what the children understand by the word strange and what would make a class strange. Would the children tell the teacher what to do? Would there be no work to do? Would the class be held on a train or a boat or outdoors? Discuss what it would be like if their parents came to their class in a reversal of roles.

Starting point

Discuss the games the children play in the playground and then go out for half an hour to play these games with your class. Talk about co-operation and friendship.

Other writing ideas

Some story themes are *The fight; The accident; The bully.* Talk about rough play, selfishness, what constitutes bullying, and the types of game that cause accidents in the playground. Take a walk round the neighbourhood to identify potential accident spots such as electricity substations, pylons, canals, railways, roads, etc. Warn the children against entering or playing games near such places.

The sheets can also be used as personal vocabulary sheets, or, after discussion, to build up charts recording impressions of playground life. Children can work in groups to do this.

Display idea

Make one enlargement of the sheet and build up the 'playground life' chart as a class activity. Get the children to add more illustrations.

Start with one word.

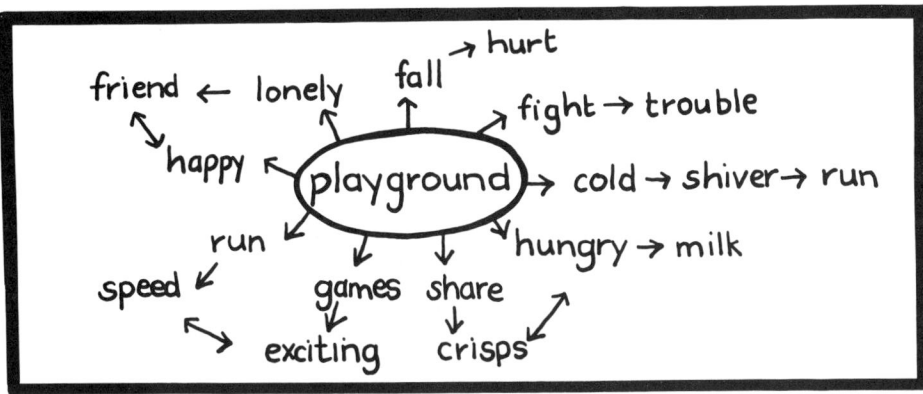

Starting point

This topic needs to be handled carefully but it will arouse the children's interest and produce worthwhile work.

Discuss the children's friends and what they like about them. Talk about the things they do together and the qualities they look for in a friend. The children can write a description of a friend and the reason they like him or her. On the sheet the children can colour one figure as themselves and one as the friend and draw a shared activity on the table between them.

Other writing ideas

Suitable subjects for stories would be *My friend the alien; My friend the robot; My friend the teddy* (or other toy). To provide stimulus, ask the children to bring in the toys or make junk models of aliens and robots. If possible, watch extracts from the film *ET*.

Starting point

Discuss things children do with their parents, e.g. gardening, shopping, washing the car, decorating, swimming, playing games, etc. Children choose one parent to write about and say what they enjoy doing together and why. Give the children time to explore the idea in the home corner where they can pretend to be a parent in different situations.

Other writing ideas

The busiest day I ever had would be a good theme, or perhaps the children are raising money for a special reason – what could they do to earn some money quickly?

9   GOING SHOPPING ▶

Starting point

Make a class shop as part of your maths work; the children can bring in containers and cartons. Discuss what happens on the weekly trip to the supermarket or local shops. Then the children can write about this.

Other writing ideas

The children could write about a Christmas shopping trip; discuss first what they would like to buy for different people. Talk about shopping lists as well, and make one together. Then the children can write one of these lists for themselves: *Things to buy for a birthday party; Things to buy for a teddy bears' picnic* or *Things to buy for a witches' tea-party*.

As an extension to this, organise a class party, perhaps using another sheet as the invitation, e.g. the teddy bear (sheet 41), the birthday cake (sheet 21) or the witch (sheet 22).

10   OUT FOR THE DAY ▶

Starting point

Discuss recent family or school outings. The children could bring in brochures, photos and other souvenirs of their trip and then write an account of it.

Other writing ideas

The theme *An imaginary school trip* would allow children to write about a trip they would like to take with their friends. Some alternatives are *The car that drove itself; Breakdown!; Lost in the fog; The time my Mum/ Dad learnt to drive.* To arouse interest the children could bring in remote-control cars.

The sheet could also be used as a personal record of vocabulary related to trips and transport.

Display idea

Make a big wall frieze and/or display individual sheets.

activity paper

To give a 3D effect, staple one side into place first and then bend the coach out slightly before stapling the other side.

pale blue activity paper at base

coloured activity paper

Child draws own background.

white paper

11   A VERY MESSY DAY ▶

Starting point

Wait until you have had a really messy time at school, e.g. with spilled milk, sand or paint. Talk about the event and what caused it. Stress the importance of tidying up and working together. The children can then write a report of the disaster, or of a messy day they have had at home.

Other writing ideas

A good subject is *A messy day at the sweet factory.* As a stimulus, read extracts from *Charlie and the Chocolate Factory* by Roald Dahl. You could make sweets or toffee with a group or the whole class, provided the safety precautions are adequate and you explain the dangers of cookers, hot pans, etc.

Two other possible subjects are *School in a pickle* and *We had a little visitor.* The former allows the children to imagine the worst possible mess that could occur in school. For the latter you may be able to arrange for a parent to bring a crawling baby or toddler (or a dog!) into class to play. The results should inspire the children.

Starting point

Make a video compilation of short clips from children's TV programmes and have a quiz or guessing game to try and find out the names of the programmes. For older children, make an audio version of the tape with theme tunes and have a team quiz. This should stimulate discussion. Make a graph of the favourite TV programmes of your class or widen the research to the whole school. Older children can write about the results of the survey; younger children can write a little about their favourite programme and why they like it.

Other writing ideas

Try writing 'the news'. Make a 'television set' from a large box and let the children experiment with the idea. You may even be able to visit a local TV studio.

Narrative pieces could include *Inside the TV* (children imagine jumping into the set and joining in the story, adverts, etc.); and *A famous visitor* (a character walks out of the TV set and joins in family life).

Display idea

Decorate a large box as a television set and mount the children's work on all four sides. Stand the 'set' on a small table in a place where the class can walk around it.

Stick on a picture.

Starting point

Discuss the children's pets, the pets' lifestyles, the reasons why the children love their animals, and any adventures they have had together. Ask the children to describe their pets, e.g. 'My rabbit likes to eat vegetables. He lives in a hutch in the garden', etc. Those children who do not have a pet can be encouraged to decide which one they would like to have and why.

Other writing ideas

Story lines could be *The lost dog* (cat/bird/alligator/giant spider, etc.); *The magician's pet shop*; *The magic dog food* (cat/bird/fish food). The latter would provide

an opportunity to stress the importance of not giving strange foods to animals.

Use the sheets also as personal vocabulary records and for blank-verse impressions of pets, for example:

The furriest friend I ever had.
Warm, soft.
Always there to welcome me home.
Quiet, pleased and purring,
my cat Freddy.

Finally, use the sheets for 'animal' charts and word play. For this the children could work in groups.

Children draw a pet of their choice.

WHEN I WAS ILL

Starting point

Discuss illnesses the children have had; what they feel like and what they do when they are ill, and who looks after them. They can then write about their experiences of being ill.

Other writing ideas

Possible story subjects are *A visit to hospital* (could be as a patient or as a visitor); *A very mysterious rash; Playing at 'doctors and nurses'.*

A parent who works or has worked in the health industry may be willing to come in (wearing uniform, if appropriate) and talk to the class. A local G.P. may even find time to visit, and the Ambulance Service will sometimes bring an ambulance to school for liaison purposes. Make the home corner into a hospital and let the children act out the roles about which they have learned.

Use the sheets, too, as personal vocabulary records.

DRESSING UP

Starting point

The children should already have experience of dressing up, at home or at school. As initial stimulus for the writing, dress three or four children as different characters – e.g. nurse, cowboy, fireman, doctor, fairy – whilst you talk to the children. Put some story books containing these characters in your book corner, e.g. *Fireman Sam* by Rob Lee (World International Ltd), *Captain Pugwash* by John Ryan (Bodley Head).

The children can write an account of their dressing up or a description of their favourite outfits.

Other writing ideas

Say to the children, 'One day something happened and you became the person you dressed up as . . . what would you do?' The story of this could be called *The day I turned into a pirate* (fireman, fairy, wizard, etc.).

Display idea

Convert the home corner into a dress shop.

A RAINY DAY

Starting point

Wait for a rainy day and take a short walk. Watch rain coursing down the windows and have raindrop races. The children can write about their impressions, likes and dislikes about wet weather.

Other writing ideas

Make umbrella mobiles from the sheets, decorating them with patterns and with faces on the handles. On other sheets the children can write the story of *The talking umbrella,* after discussion about what the umbrella might want to say and whether it has any magic powers. Finished versions of the stories could be copied onto the reverse sides of the decorated mobile ones.

Other stories could be about *The flying umbrella* or *The wizard's umbrella.* Discuss where a flying umbrella might take the children; invent magic lands such as 'Rainland' or 'The land of toys'; and read extracts from *The faraway tree* by Enid Blyton. For the wizard's umbrella, bring in an old umbrella, keep it closed and fill it with small items such as scarves, paper beads, toys, shells, etc. Pretend to be the wizard and pull the things out one by one. Encourage the children to talk about magic powers and what the umbrella can do.

Use the sheets also for word play and for personal vocabulary records. Older children could write blank-verse impressions of rain.

Staple to ceiling.

raindrops of
silver paper
(art foil)

cotton

Mount each umbrella on activity paper.
Hang it from the ceiling on a strip of
crepe paper of the same colour or on
a strip of cellophane.

Hang clouds
and rainbows
on brackets.

children's
writing

rough strips of cellophane

silver-foil puddle

Starting point

Wait for a snowy day or the day after a snowy weekend. Discuss the fun the children had in the snow. Talk about how it sounded and felt and how everywhere looked different. If it is snowy at school, let the children go out to play, build a snowman, have snowball fights, etc. The children can write about their play or their impressions of the snow.

Other writing ideas

Watch video material about the wildlife and environment in snowy lands, or about winter sports. The children could write on either of these subjects; or they could write an adventure story – *Lost in the snow* – in which someone (it could be the child) is lost, or deliberately left behind, or thrown by magic into a land of snow. Retell *The snowman* by Raymond Briggs to catch the children's imaginations.

The sheets could also be used as personal vocabulary records; for a letter to or from Father Christmas; as a base for a calendar or Christmas card; and, for older children, for blank-verse impressions of snow.

Display idea

Cut out hats from activity paper of assorted colours.

white doilies   silver-foil   white paint   dark blue activity paper

white paper

Scarves are coloured by children.

When mounting, curve the snowmen out slightly.

Starting point

Wait for a frosty day and take a walk outside to look at branches, earth, walls, leaves, etc. Look at slides in the playground, ice on puddles, frosty patterns on windows, and breath on the frosty air. Warn about the dangers of ice on roads, slides on pavements and thin ice on ponds. The children can write about their impressions of the day.

Other writing ideas

Discuss what Jack Frost might look like, where he would live, what might happen if he came indoors and why he might want to come in. Then the children can write about Jack Frost.

Use the sheet also as a personal vocabulary record, and, for older children, for word play and blank verse about the weather, danger, beauty, etc.

drawing of a bare branch

Starting point

Wait for a hot day and discuss what it feels like to be hot and what heat is. Talk about how to get cool. Discuss the things the children like to do on a hot day, such as playing in a paddling pool or with a hosepipe, and going on trips and picnics. Go and play outside for ten minutes after the discussion and then, possibly, have a cool drink before starting writing. The children can write about their favourite activities and likes and dislikes associated with hot days.

Other writing ideas

The giant ice-lolly would be a good topic. Try and make a giant ice-lolly as a scientific experiment. Discuss moulds, size of freezer, sticks, etc. The children's story could include a mad inventor. Another story – *The everlasting ice-lolly* – could be about a lolly with special powers, made by a wizard.

Wait for a sunny day and then go outside and experiment with shadows. Play chasing games and have puppet shows. The children can write a story about their shadows, which can talk and like ice-lollies – *Me and my shadow.*

Display ideas

Cut black shadow figures from paper and display them along the wall or hang them from the ceiling. Each figure holds an ice-lolly. Or you could make a lolly stall.

Mount lollies on coloured activity paper and suspend with matching crepe paper.

SIDE VIEW

Rolled paper bent centrally holds the canopy about 6 inches from the wall.

Starting point

Wait for a windy day and go outside to feel the wind and watch clouds, smoke, washing, trees and leaves blowing in the wind. Discuss impressions and feelings. Ask the children to bring in kites, or make kites as part of your art and craft work. The children can write about the fun they had playing out in the wind.

Other writing ideas

Retell the story of the sun and the wind battling with the traveller. The children can write the tale in their own words.

The children could write about *The wind from the other side of the world* – a strange wind that comes one day and blows the most unusual things into the garden. Discuss first where the wind might come from, what it carries with it and what, if anything, stops it.

Use the sheet also as a personal vocabulary record and, with older children, for word play.

Display idea

Hang an assortment of weather stories near a winter tableau or frieze.

Starting point

Hold a class discussion about birthdays. Ask the children to bring in presents and cards from their last birthday. Set up a birthday party in the home corner, providing a pretend cake, cards, paper for wrapping and old toys as presents. The children can write about their own birthday experiences or their play in the home corner.

Other writing ideas

Use the sheet as a party invitation and decorate the cake accordingly. Various parties are possible:

A teddy bears' party with a cake decorated with sugar, bees and honey pots.

A goblins' party with a slimy cake decorated with toads, snails, beetles, etc.

A pirates' party with a cake decorated with a skull and crossbones, flags, cutlasses and maps about treasure.

The invitation should say when and where the party will take place, e.g. at midnight in Strange Wood, by the light of the new moon.

Display idea

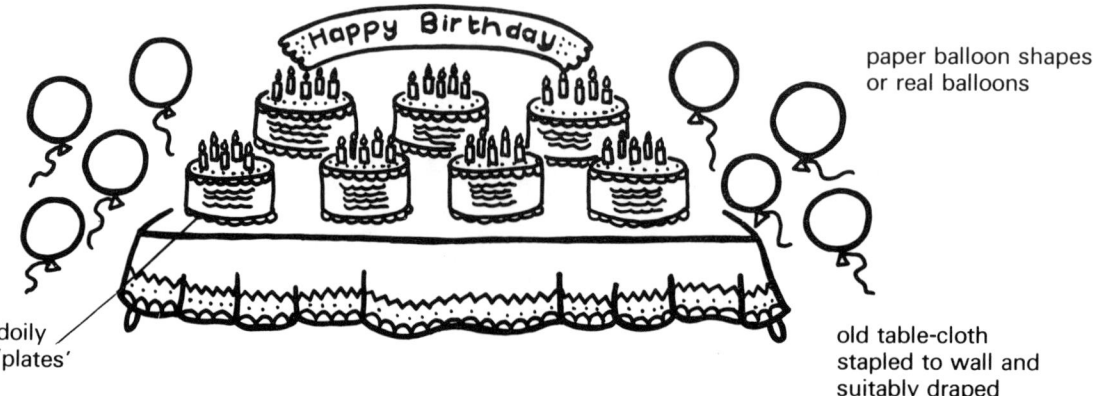

paper balloon shapes or real balloons

doily 'plates'

old table-cloth stapled to wall and suitably draped

Starting point

For the initial stimulus sing songs about witches (see *Harlequin,* published by A & C Black), read 'witchy' stories, and perhaps get someone to dress up as a witch while you discuss the activity. Younger children can write about a Hallowe'en party at home, or one you have held in class, with such activities as duck apple (apple bobbing).

Other writing ideas

Possible story themes are *The witch's cat; Trick or Treat; The giant pumpkin house.*

The sheet could be used in other ways too: to write a recipe for a Hallowe'en cooking lesson (pumpkin pie, toffee apples, parkin, etc.); for a menu for a witches' party; for a spell; for an invitation to a Hallowe'en party; for a letter from a witch to a friend.

Display ideas

You can make some very striking displays, like those shown here. Give the children appropriate shapes on which to write spells and position these over an enlargement of the cauldron.

Mount witches in a woodland scene.

silver-foil

Children colour these.

black paper or paint

grey or blue activity paper

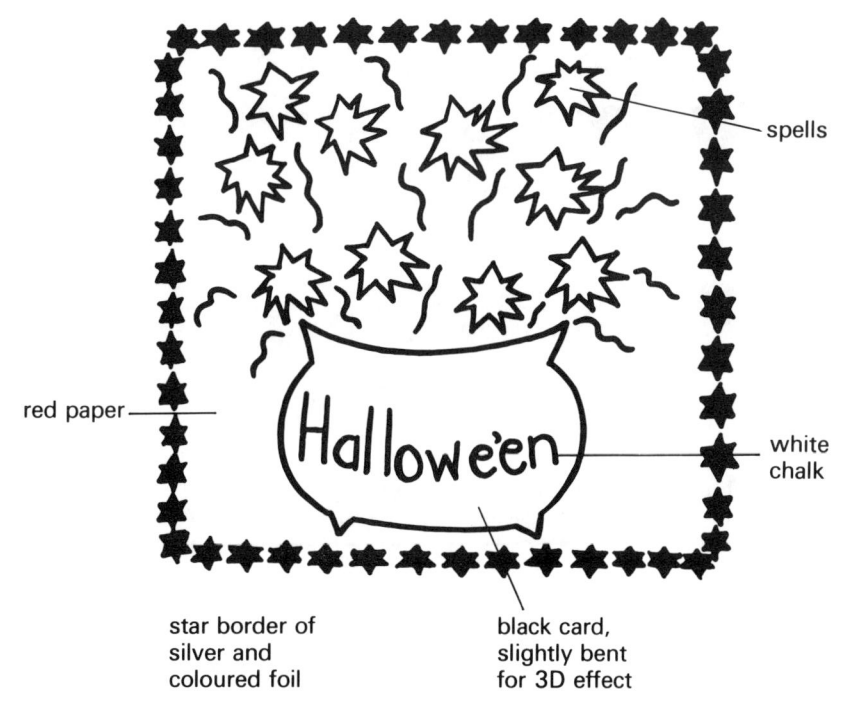

spells

red paper

white chalk

star border of silver and coloured foil

black card, slightly bent for 3D effect

silver-foil

children's writing

black

blue and white

red sky

black

Hallowe'en is coming!

black activity paper

Staple at one side, then bend out slightly to give 3-D effect before stapling second edge.

red, orange or yellow cellophane behind holes

23   BONFIRE NIGHT

Starting point

As preparation for this subject, and well before the event, talk about the safety aspects of the night. After the event, discuss the experiences the children had and let them paint pictures of fireworks and bonfires. The children can write about what they did or did not do on the night.

Other writing ideas

Make a warning poster about the dangers of fire and fireworks. For reception-class children, you will have to

write a basic warning (e.g. Keep away from fire; Don't touch matches), but the children can colour the poster. If any children can under-write (copy) the warning, let them do so; this will help them to begin to see that writing can warn, inform, alert, etc. Older children can write their own captions.

The sheet could also be used to advertise a bonfire party; as an invitation; as a personal vocabulary record; and for word play. Complete the flame shapes and write the words with fire-coloured crayons.

Display idea

Starting point

Read or retell the story of the birth of Christ and look at drawings or paintings of the Nativity. In addition to this, your school or class may be involved in the production of a Nativity play. The children can retell the story or write about their impressions of it.

Other writing ideas

The sheet would make a good basis for an advertisement or programme for the school Christmas concert, play or carol service. Also, with the bottom cut off and the top mounted on card, it can be used for Christmas cards. The children draw in their own versions of the figures in the Christmas story. Finally, it can be used as a personal vocabulary sheet.

Starting point

The children will probably be sufficiently interested already, but if not, read stories from *Stories for Christmas* by Alison Uttley (Puffin).

The children can write a story about what Father Christmas does on Christmas Eve or about what their family does during the Christmas holiday, e.g. going to church, Christmas dinner, present giving, visiting relatives, eating festive foods.

Other writing ideas

Some story ideas are *The day the sleigh broke down; The lost reindeer; The night before Christmas.*

The sheet can also be used in these ways: for listing the presents the children would like for Christmas and those they would like to give; as an invitation to a party or the school play or concert; as an advertisement for the play/concert; as Father Christmas's advertisement for helpers; for instructions for a party game or food; for a letter to or from Father Christmas.

Display idea

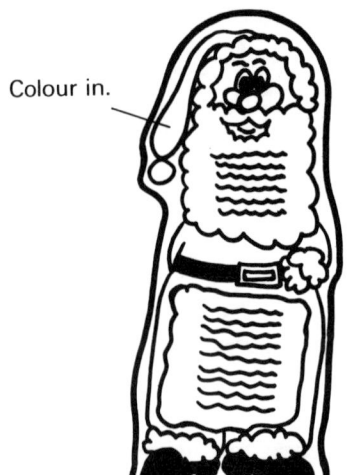

Colour in.

Mount on red activity paper.

Add very light cotton-wool hair and fur.

edging of cotton-wool round writing

Colour a border of red round writing (mark with pencil first).

For posters, fill in the beard and write on the skirt.

Starting point

Take a walk round school, inside and outside, looking for signs of spring. Visit the local park or nearby countryside. Use this sheet as the base for an I-spy record. Make a list of the changes and then let the children write about their own observations.

Other writing ideas

To interest the children in writing a story about *Spring-cleaning day at our house* have a spring-clean of the classroom or the home corner. Discuss what funny things might happen at home, e.g. the cat keeps getting into the cupboards.

Other story themes could be: *The Easter story* – retell the story of the first Easter and then let the children write it in their own words; *The strange egg* – about a magic Easter egg which contains a fairy creature, or a 'real' egg that hatches into something unusual. The egg itself could be oddly shaped and coloured. To prepare for writing about *The Easter bunny's big surprise,* talk to the children about what surprises they and their families like. The story could be about a meeting with the Easter bunny to arrange a family surprise.

Use the sheet also for topic work on the seasons, as a personal vocabulary record. Any of the 'seasonal' sheets can be used for a letter to parents about school events falling within the relevant period, e.g. autumn fayre, harvest festival, school visit to a nature reserve, spring concert.

Display idea

This idea will help the children learn about periods of time.

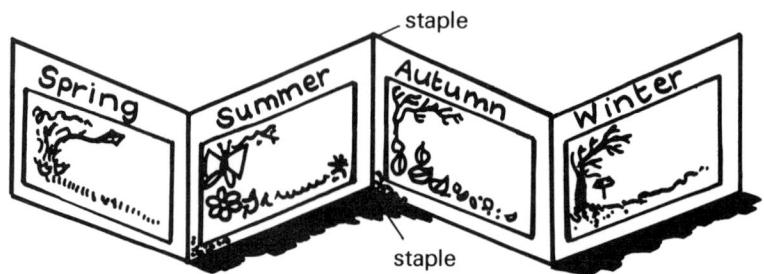

Mount sheets on activity paper of 4 different seasonal colours. Build up a zig-zag book. Display it at the end of the school year.

SUMMER ▶

Starting point

Discuss activities the children like to do in summer, e.g. going on a school trip to the seaside or to a nature reserve; environmental studies. Ask the children to bring in hobbies equipment, e.g. for camping, walking and swimming. Bring in summer flowers for the classroom. Look for signs of summer in school, e.g. lessons outside, trips, open windows, playtime on the grass.

The children can write about a trip, or the games they like to play in summer, or about their impressions of summer.

Other writing ideas

Read stories about summer activities and then let the children write their own: *My summer holidays; The giant sunflower; There's something at the bottom of my garden; The magic sunhat; The flower fairies.*

Use the sheet also for verses, word play and as a personal vocabulary record.

29

AUTUMN ▶

Starting point

Go for a walk in woodland if possible. Look out for indications of change in the season as you go. Look around school for changes too, e.g. warm radiators, condensation on the windows. Make a collection of natural objects such as twigs, bulbs, leaves, horse chestnuts, berries, nuts, fruits. The children can write about their impressions of the weather and the changes they have seen, or about how they enjoyed the walk. Talk about autumn games such as 'conkers'.

Other writing ideas

Talk about hibernation and read stories about animal life in autumn. The children could then write about *A woodland adventure* or *The squirrels' secret store.* Or they could write an adventure story called *Lost in the leaves.*

Use the sheet also as a personal vocabulary record, and with older children, for verses and word play.

30

WINTER ▶

Starting point

Go for a walk round school, inside and outside. Note the signs of winter, e.g. scarves, boots and gloves in the cloakroom. Discuss winter hobbies (indoor and outdoor) and watch video extracts of winter sports and the landscape in winter. Discuss outdoor games that keep you warm and go out to play for a short time. The children can write about this or about their impressions of winter weather. The sheet can be coloured as a snowy picture or as a wet, muddy landscape.

Other writing ideas

Some possible story themes are: *Adventure on the coldest day of the year; The hungry robin; Accident on the ice; The next-door neighbour* (who could be old, cold and lonely; a practical joker; etc.).

Use the sheet also as a personal vocabulary record, for verse and for word play.

CINDERELLA ▶

Starting point

Read or tell the story. Bring in a velvet cushion and a pair of glittery evening shoes. Use this sheet or the scroll on sheet 63 to make a large invitation to the ball. The children can retell the story.

Other writing ideas

Use the sheet for the Ugly Sisters' shopping list, for a letter from the Prince to Cinderella after they have found out that the slipper fits her, or as a poster for the school pantomime.

Starting point

Read or tell the story. Bring in a small basket containing a rosy apple, a comb and a ribbon. Use this, with a shawl and scarf for the Wicked Queen's disguise as a pedlar (a child could dress up as you tell the story). Decorate an old standing mirror as the magic mirror and let the children 'try it out'. Then the children can write the story in their own words.

Other writing ideas

The sheet can be used for many different forms of writing – the Wicked Queen's spell for poison; a letter from Snow White to the Huntsman, thanking him for sparing her; a day's menu for the Seven Dwarfs (three meals); descriptions of the dwarfs, Queen, Prince, etc.

old bathroom mirror

Decorate with coloured foil stars, bolts of lightening and coils of foil, stuck on with Copydex.

Starting point

Read or tell the story. Bring in three teddy bears of different sizes, and change the home corner into the Bears' cottage by adding three chairs, bowls, spoons and beds. Let the children retell the story.

Other writing ideas

Discuss what behaviour is considered to be bad and relate it to Goldilocks' behaviour. Then the children could write a letter from the Bears to Goldilocks' parents complaining about their child's behaviour, and an apologetic letter from Goldilocks.

Write an advertisement for the Bears' brand of porridge, stressing its special properties – ensures glossy coat, cold nose, strong claws, etc. For this activity ask the children to bring in various cereal packets so that you can look at the advertising material.

Starting point

Read or tell the story. Bring in a basket and put in it one or two treats for sick grandparents. Ask the children to suggest what their grandparents would like. Make a cloak and hood from red crepe paper and let one of the children wear it while you read the story. You could also make one from material and let the children use it for more rigorous play in the home corner. Provide a shawl and wolf's ears. The children can write the story in their own words.

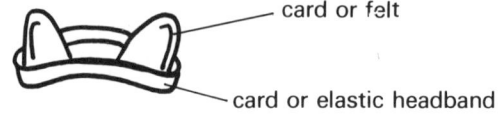

card or felt

card or elastic headband

Other writing ideas

Write the Huntsman's or the Wolf's account of what happened. Make a warning poster about the dangerous Wolf. Talk about 'stranger danger' in real life.

THE PARK

Starting point

Go on a visit to the local park. Make a large wall picture in the classroom and put on it all the things you saw and even things you would like to see, e.g. flower beds, ponds, benches, space slides, tennis courts, football pitches, see-saws. Point out dangers to the children when you are at the park. The children can write about the trip, or about an experience they have had at another time.

Other writing ideas

The children could write about the kind of park they would like near their house – *The super park.*

Display idea

climbing frame made from rolled activity paper

We went to the park to play.

children's own paintings, cut out and stapled on

36

THE FAIR

Starting point

If possible visit a local fair or pleasure park. Try to obtain the BBC's programme *Q.E.D.* about fairgrounds, which is available on video. The children can write about the fun they had, about favourite rides, fears and other feelings.

Other writing ideas

An adventure story would be appropriate – *Stuck at the top of the big wheel; Lost in the ghost-train tunnel;* or *The fair that came to life at midnight.*

37

THE ZOO

Starting point

Get some pictures and posters of zoo animals and, if possible, visit a nearby zoo. You could make an I-spy book from this sheet to use on the trip. Ask the children to bring in toy zoo animals and set up a model zoo in the classroom. There are many Wildlife videos on the market and the children would benefit from seeing short extracts. The children can write a report of their trip or a description of an animal they like, e.g. 'I like the lions because they have smooth brown fur'.

Other writing ideas

Talk about what might happen if the lions escaped or at the chimps' tea-party. Perhaps the lions would meet an incredible lion-tamer, or a sheepdog; perhaps the chimps would get up to mischief at the tea-party. Let the children write about what happens in one of the situations.

SOMETHING UNDER THE BED

Starting point

Discuss the children's fears about strange places and night-time noises, darkness and being alone. Discuss, in a lighthearted way, what sort of thing could be under the bed and what they could do about it. Talk about methods of communicating with the 'outside world' (i.e. 'down-stairs') and possible escape plans.

The children can have great fun with this topic, but handle it carefully and make sure that nervous children are not frightened and that they do not leave school with lingering fears.

Starting point

Prepare the children the day before the sheet is to be used by discussing bath-time activities and games – and disasters! Talk about the toys the children play with and allow them to bring in one favourite toy on the day you use the sheet. Ask them to try and have a specially good bath time, in preparation for the next day. The children can then write about their experiences.

Other writing ideas

This topic is ideal for imaginative writing and you can have a lively time during preparation time. For *When I went down the plughole* discuss what happens to the water. Discuss size and shape and the possible event that made the child small enough to fit down the plughole, e.g. magic soap, strange shampoo. For *Trapped in a bubble* provide bubble liquid and let the children observe and play with the bubbles. Discuss how they might get trapped, the adventure and the escape. Other themes could be *Mum's/Dad's disaster with the bubbles; The day the water went purple; It wasn't me who left the tap running.*

Display idea

Make bubbles and suspend them around a classroom display.

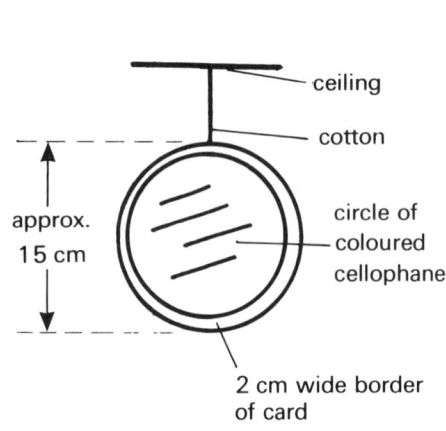

ceiling

cotton

approx. 15 cm

circle of coloured cellophane

2 cm wide border of card

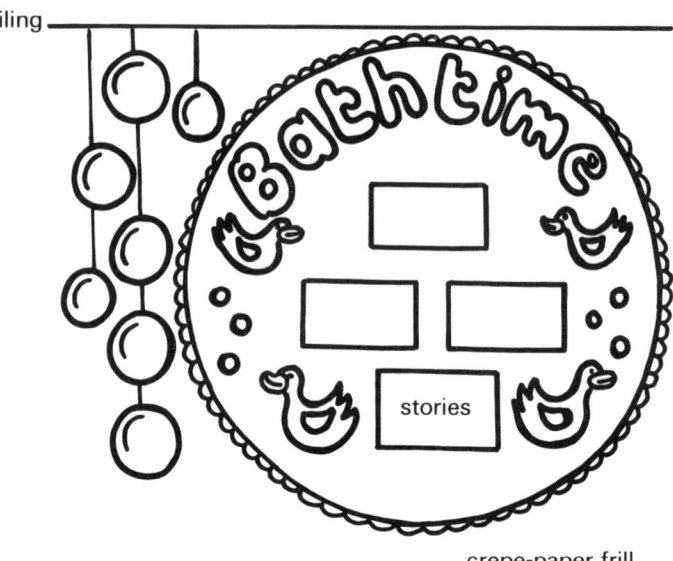

ceiling

stories

crepe-paper frill

Starting point

Bring in pictures and posters of different occupations and, if possible, invite one or two people into school, e.g. nurse, police officer, fireman, shop assistant, engineer, etc. Discuss things the children enjoy doing and the skills they think they have. They may already have some ideas about what they want to be when they grow up – let them write about these.

Starting point

Read some bear stories, e.g. *Teddy Robinson* by Joan Robinson (Young Puffin), *Paddington Bear* by Michael Bond (Armada Lion), *Super Ted* by Mike Young (Random House). The children can each bring in their own bear (if they have one) on the day you use the sheet. Discuss places and events leading up to the disappearance of teddy, and how the children would feel. The children can then write the adventure with whatever conclusion (sad or happy) they think fit. Let the children colour in the teddy on the sheet to look like their own (or one they would like to have), adding any special markings, clothes, etc. Use sheet 65 (the 'wanted' poster) to advertise for the lost bear.

Other writing ideas

The children could write an adventure about one of the teddy heroes they have read about. Or they could write a description of their own bear: why they love teddy, when they got him/her. Finally, let the children invent a new teddy hero or heroine and invest it with whatever powers they can think of.

Display idea

Mount on toning activity paper.

Cut out and colour extra heads and bodies.

pale blue activity paper

Wanted

Wanted

Lost teddy

Use the 'Wanted' poster on sheet 65.

cut-out story teddies

green activity paper

brown activity paper for old cardboard boxes

pale blue crepe frill

---

42 | SPECIAL MACHINE ▶

Starting point

Read part of *Charlie and the chocolate factory* by Roald Dahl to give the children an idea of one type of special machine. Talk about what they would want their special machine to make, what raw materials they would need, what power source it would use (e.g. magic, steam, water,

nuclear). Use your art and craft lessons to let the children make junk models of the machine. Decide on a class machine and let the children make the various parts. They can then write an adventure involving the machine, or an account of how they made the machine.

---

43 | SPACE JOURNEY ▶

Starting point

Use a video compilation of current TV space stories (fact and fiction). Write to NASA, Cape Canaveral, USA for a topic pack on the space shuttle. Ask children to bring in space toys and make a diorama. Collect books and comics so that the children can copy pictures. Turn the home corner into a space station. The children can write about

life on the space station or about the journey out into space, and use another sheet to draw the scene on the planet they visit.

Other writing ideas

Suggested story titles are: *Life on the planet Saturn; The space school.*

---

44 | 45 | ALIEN ▶

Starting point

Watch extracts from suitable TV programmes and from the film *ET*. Discuss the idea of alien life, what the children's alien might look like and what in its home environment has caused it to look as it does, e.g. it may be camouflaged for life on a planet of glass, fire, or dense jungle. Discuss attitudes towards strangers, differences and possible difficulties in communication. Get the children to make models of the aliens in clay, or to make a material collage. They can write a description of the alien

and/or an account of how they met and how the alien got to Earth or the child into space.

Other writing ideas

Story themes could include *Monster from the deep; The thing under the bed; They came to rule the world.*

Display idea

For sheets 42, 43, 44 and 45. (See overleaf.)

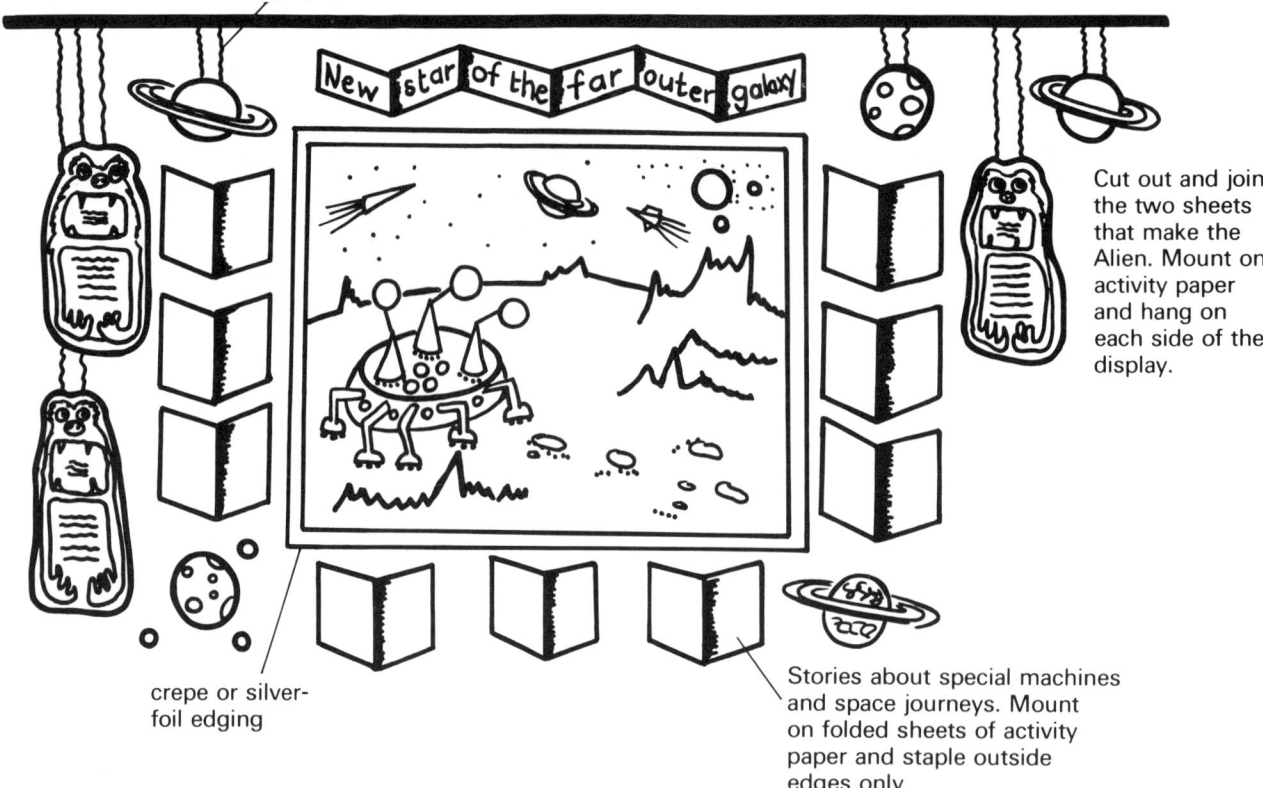

crepe paper to tone with planet

Fold title in gentle zig-zag.

New star of the far outer galaxy

Cut out and join the two sheets that make the Alien. Mount on activity paper and hang on each side of the display.

crepe or silver-foil edging

Stories about special machines and space journeys. Mount on folded sheets of activity paper and staple outside edges only.

46 | FAIRIES IN OUR HOUSE ▶

Starting point

Find a large selection of books on fairies and fairy stories and read some of them, e.g. *The elves and the shoemaker*. Discuss what characteristics fairies have, e.g. they have magical powers, are small with wings, and carry wands. Discuss the possibility of fairies being good or evil and what sort of things they can do, according to fairy stories. Talk about the arrival of the fairies in the children's homes – how they came to be there, what they did, whether they communicated with the family or just with the pets or the children. The visitors could be relations of the Christmas-tree fairy or the tooth fairy, or maybe they came out of a book. As further stimulus, put cellophane wings on the dolls in the home corner and give them wands. The children can write about a fairy friend or the arrival of mischievous fairies in the house.

Other writing ideas

Story themes could be *The day we shrank; The story that came to life.*

47 | 48 | GIANT CATERPILLAR ▶

Starting point

Talk about the life-cycle of the butterfly, illustrated by pictures. If possible, visit a butterfly farm. Read *The very hungry caterpillar* by Eric Carle (Puffin). Discuss the possibilities of such a giant creature: its exact size, eating habits, the damage it could do, e.g. eating trees, squashing cars. Think what could be done about it. Would it turn into a giant butterfly and lay giant eggs? The children can write the adventure story.

Give each child the two sheets so that he/she can have a long caterpillar. If the child is not likely to write a long story let him/her draw a pattern on the remaining segments, or make sure that the writing is well spaced out. The two sheets can be mounted and folded at each segment. If you wish to make a wider page, for younger children to write on, cover up the segment lines on the sheet before photocopying.

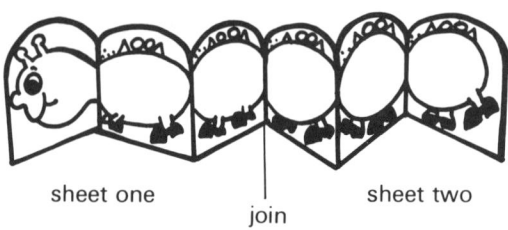

sheet one   join   sheet two

Display idea

Mount the stories as zig-zag books. These can be stood on surfaces or stapled to the wall in zig-zag form – possibly on a garden frieze.

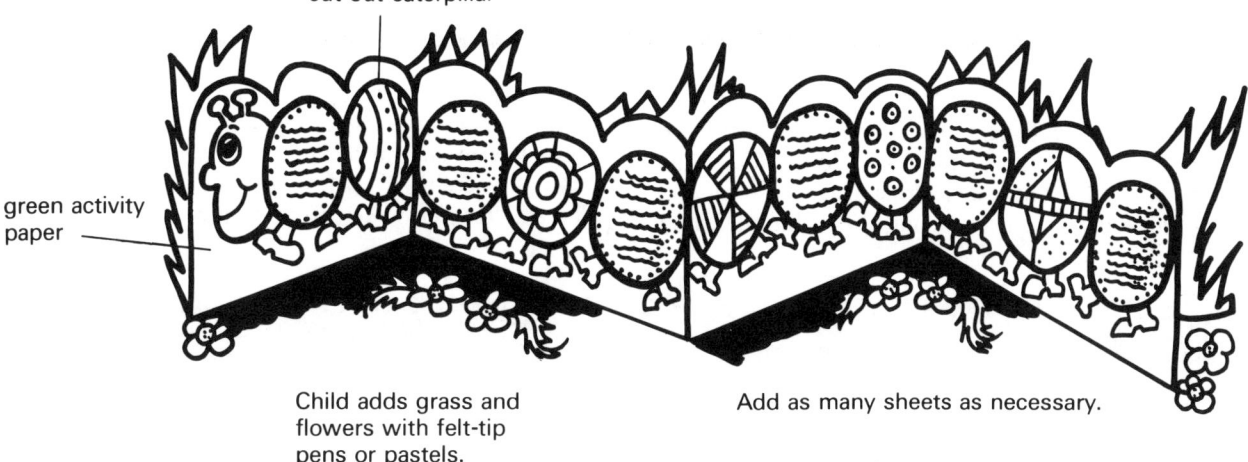

cut-out caterpillar

green activity paper

Child adds grass and flowers with felt-tip pens or pastels.

Add as many sheets as necessary.

49 HAUNTED HOUSE

Starting point

Watch a video compilation of extracts from films and current TV programmes about ghosts, or read *Funny Bones* by Janet and Allan Ahlberg (Armada Lion). Discuss what the children know of ghosts and haunted houses. Talk about general fears and dislikes and frightening things. Talk about what ghosts look like and use one sheet to draw the ghost(s) in the house. Let the children write a description of the ghost or an adventure in which they are instrumental in getting rid of the ghost or making friends with it. Maybe the ghost stays for a long time!

Other writing ideas

The sheet can be used for a Hallowe'en story.

Display idea

ghosts cut from white paper

large house made from activity paper

black paper

hinge   loose body

Stick the upper part of each ghost to the black backing and then staple a 'hinge' firmly across each shape. The children's writings are mounted and 'hidden' beneath the loose, flapping, ghostly bodies.

25

Starting point

Bring in a colourful rug and read some of the *Arabian Nights* stories. Discuss journeys and decide where the magic carpet might have come from; maybe it was found in an old house that once belonged to a traveller from Arabia. Talk about magic words and how the children might discover the carpet's power. It may have other magic powers such as being able to talk or grant wishes. Discuss where the carpet might take the new traveller. The children can write this adventure story.

Starting point

Watch the film *Swiss Family Robinson* (Walt Disney) or read the shipwreck passage from the book, which was written by Johann Wyss. Video material of the Tudor ship *Mary Rose* and the Swedish warship *Wasa* is available and children would benefit from watching the underwater scenes. Bring in models and pictures of ships and boats. Discuss what it might be like to be involved in a shipwreck or to go scuba diving and discover a wreck. The children can write about either of these.

Other writing ideas

Appropriate themes for narratives would be *Cast away on a desert island; Treasure hunting; The monster in the wreck.*

Starting point

Watch extracts from the films *Miranda the mermaid* with Glynis Johns and *Splash!* with Darryl Hannah (both available on video). Read *The little mermaid* by Hans Christian Andersen or passages from *The water babies* by Charles Kingsley (cartoon versions are now available of these). Discuss the children's lifestyle and what the mermaid's might be like – sleeping, eating, school, play, clothes, etc. The mermaid may use things from the sea as everyday tools, e.g. a shell for a comb, a rock pool for a mirror, a dolphin to ride on. The children can write about the life of a mermaid or how they met one and made friends with her.

Other writing ideas

Some more story ideas are: *I turned into a mermaid; The mermaid who came to visit; The deep-sea fishing trip.*

Display idea

children's stories in shells

Starting point

Discuss the moral issues involved in honesty, fair play, cheating, telling lies. Discuss competitions and the merits of being a good competitor and winning or losing gracefully. This could be done before the school sports day. The children can write the story of someone who cheated. You may want to talk about punishment and disgrace, being sorry and wiping the slate clean, and making a new start.

Other writing ideas

Some possible themes are *Our sports day; The big race; The Olympics; The World Cup.*

Display idea

Paint the Olympic rings on a white background, mount the sheets on papers of the same colours as the rings, and pin them up as shown.

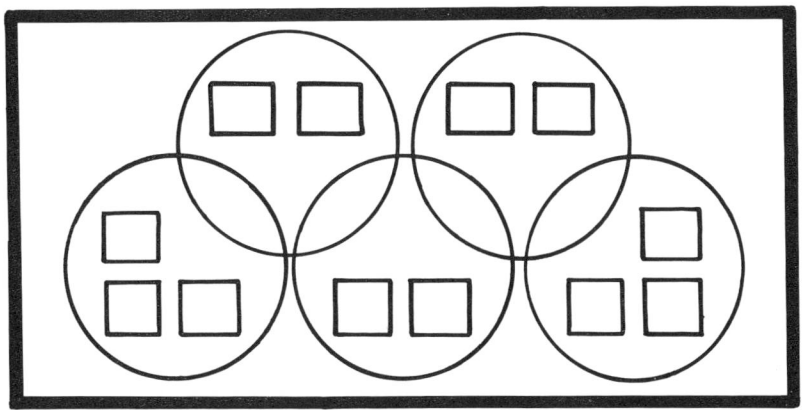

Starting point

Read one of the many dragon books on the market, e.g. *The Usborne book of dragons* (Usborne); *There's no such thing as a dragon* (Blackie); *Lo High and the dragon of winter* by J. Fitzsimmons in *Bright ideas for Easter* (Scholastic). Watch extracts on reptiles from the BBC's *Living planet* videos. Make model dragons from junk or clay or make a Chinese dragon (if there is a local Chinese community, they may be willing to help). Discuss what it would be like to meet or to own a dragon and what the relationship with it would be like. Talk about how the children would feed and house it, depending on its size.

Would it be invisible to all but children? Would it fly? Would it breathe fire? The children can write about how they made their model or they can write an adventure in which they meet a dragon.

Other writing ideas

The children can write about *A Chinese festival; The angry dragon; St George and the dragon* (retell the old story first).

Display idea

Mount dragons on a background of 'sky'.

yellow crepe frill   blue activity paper

27

Starting point

Read stories about journeys into secret places, such as *The lion, the witch and the wardrobe* by C.S. Lewis or *Alice through the looking glass* by Lewis Carroll. Discuss where the children might find a secret door and what sort of places they would like it to lead to, such as make-believe lands. The children can then try to write such a story.

Other writing ideas

Stories for this topic could be *My secret garden; The mysterious castle; Next door.*

Display ideas

Pin up the sheets as shown or make a flap-book.

children's writing

Glue the sheets together (not the door).

fold

Cut around 3 sides of door.

Use this double sheet as the cover for an A5 size story book.

Draw here what awaits behind the door.

The door will open.

28

Starting point

Visit a circus if possible. Collect posters and books containing circus stories and illustrations, and ask the children to bring in toy circus figures to make a diorama. Listen or dance to the music from *Barnum*. You could also provide clown costumes for the home corner and make clown masks in art and craft lessons. The children can write about how they felt as a clown or, if they have been to a circus, what they enjoyed about it most.

Alternatively they could write about what happens at a circus.

Other writing ideas

For *The saddest clown in the circus* talk first about why the clown might be sad and what might make him or her happy again. For *A fire at the circus* talk about how everybody could be saved.

Display ideas

Fold crepe and staple.

3 colours of crepe paper: strips 10 cm wide

To give figures a 3D effect, staple one side in place and bend out slightly before fixing the second side.

Provide a large topical picture as a stimulus to story writing. Pin it to the wall and, later, mount the completed story-clowns and hang them from crepe-paper strips on either side of the picture.

THE SEASIDE

Starting point

If possible, go on a trip to the seaside. Learn the song *Oh, I do like to be beside the seaside*. Make a large wall picture as stimulus and turn the home corner into a sun-centre, with lilos, deckchairs, sunhats, glasses, flippers, ice-creams, etc. Collect objects associated with the seaside, such as shells, nets and buckets and spades to make a display and, if possible, provide some sand play. Talk about the children's experiences at the seaside and games they like to play. They can write about this or about the play in the sun-centre.

Other writing ideas

This topic provides a wide range of story-themes – *Washed out to sea* (talk first about the dangers of boating and playing near water); *The biggest sand-castle in the world* (have a go at making sand-castles if your sand tray/pit is big enough – use damp sand); *The little talking seahorse* – the story of a child who meets a sea-horse while playing in a rock pool.

LOOKING AFTER BABY

Starting point

Talk about babies and the children's own memories or experiences of siblings, cousins or neighbouring children. Discuss what needs babies have, e.g. sleep, nappies, bottles, comfort, play; and talk about some of the problems, such as communication and feeding-time difficulties. Link this story to sheets 11 and 39, *A very messy day* and *Bath time*. Let the children choose which approach to take on the general theme of what it is like, or might be like, looking after a baby.

A parent with a baby may be willing to talk to your class about the everyday routine involved in looking after a very young child – and about the responsibilities, worries, fun and comical events. Afterwards, discuss the visit with the class. Provide the home corner with a 'baby' and ask children to bring in dolls for a baby show (the boys should join in as well!).

Other writing ideas

The children could write about *The day I turned into a baby*.

THE DREAM

Starting point

Discuss dreams and ask the children to try and remember any dreams they have had. Discuss the strange skills that are sometimes acquired in dreams, such as flying, lifting huge weights or walking over houses. Ask the children to write about a dream they have had or one they would like to have. Talk about the differences between dreams and nightmares and about the fears that sometimes come out in nightmares. Allow the children to write about these if they want to.

Other writing ideas

Popular story topics are *The dream that came true* and *But it was only a dream* (waking up after a fantastic adventure).

THE TRAIN

Starting point

Visit the local railway station and, if possible, go on a short journey. If you are near enough, go to a railway museum or model railway. Discuss the differences between monorail, underground and standard railways. Ask children to bring in model trains and set up a diorama; some children may allow others to play with their trains. Other groups can collect and display pictures and posters (travel posters are available from British Rail); and individual children can tell the class about places they have visited by train. The children can write about playing with toy trains, about a train journey or about anything else they have learned about railways.

Other writing ideas

Discuss strange lands such as those in *The Faraway Tree* by Enid Blyton. Ask the children to write about some lands that *The enchanted train* might visit, e.g. Upside-down land, Back-to-front land or The land of nursery rhymes or riddles. Other story subjects could be *The dream train; The flying train; The train that broke down; Stuck in the tunnel*.

Display idea

This is a double sheet so the children can use as many carriages as they need and have a train each. Or the class can make one long train by writing on carriages attached to the engine, which shows the title of the work.

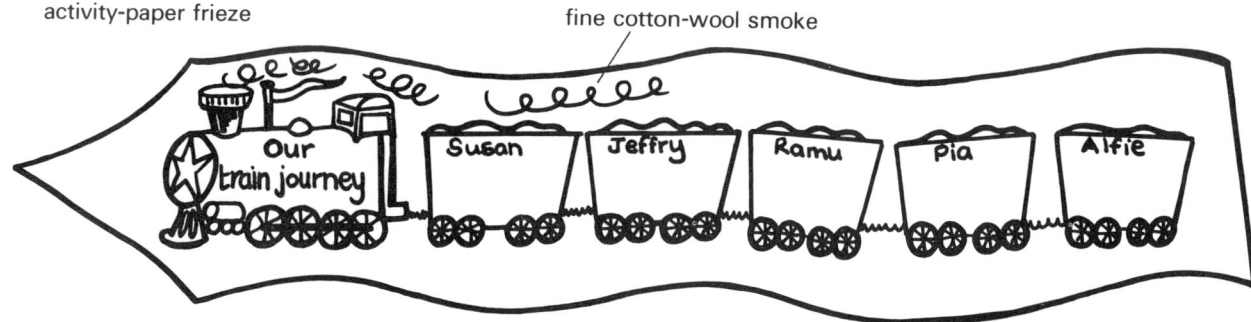

activity-paper frieze

fine cotton-wool smoke

Our train journey

Susan Jeffry Ramu Pia Alfie

A PROCLAMATION

Starting point

Use this sheet for a letter or advertisement to announce a forthcoming event at school. The children can compose and write either of these themselves.

Other writing ideas

The sheet is ideal for a fairy story, a town crier's proclamation, an historical tale, or as a certificate of merit/prize certificate.

AN OLD DOCUMENT

Starting point

Suggest that the children draw a treasure map and write a story about a treasure island. Sheet 51, *The shipwreck,* could be used in combination with this one.

Other writing ideas

A letter would be appropriate – perhaps a letter found in a bottle on the seashore, or an old letter from a storybook character or historical figure (e.g. from the Sleeping Beauty before she fell asleep).

Display idea

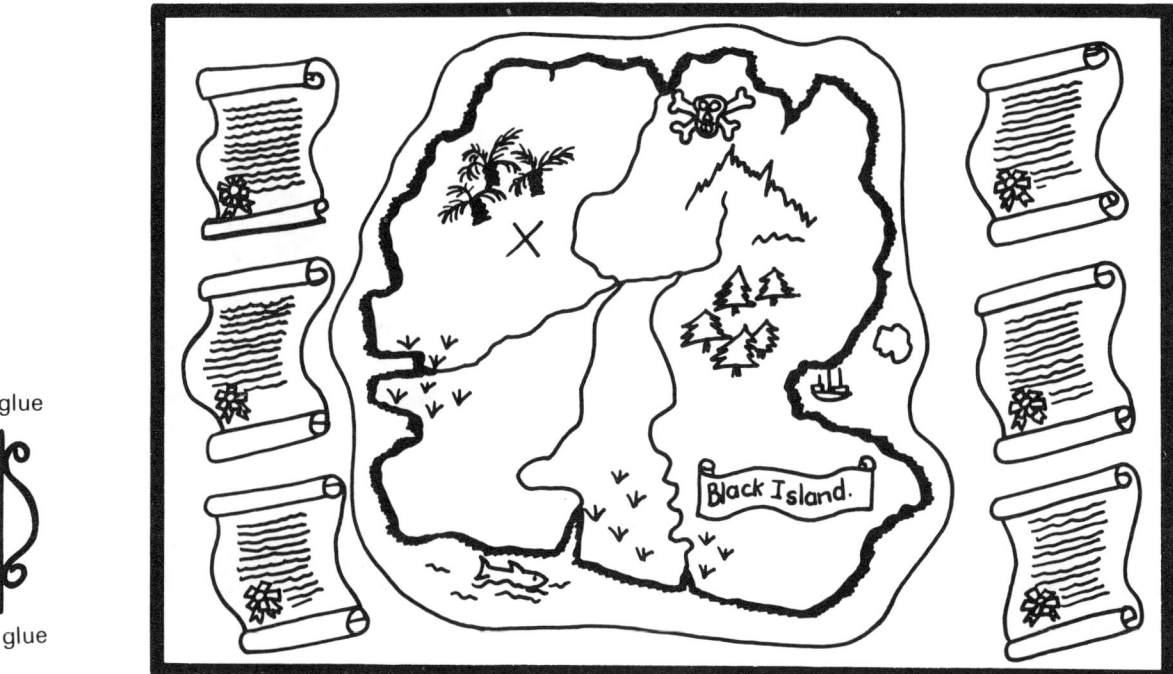

glue

glue

Black Island.

Scrolls mounted on wall in semi-3D way, bent away from wall. Side view.

Starting point

Use the sheet for descriptive writing about a person wanted for a crime, e.g. pirate, cowboy, robbers. The poster should say what the crime was.

Other writing ideas

Try an advertisement, e.g. for a court jester, a nanny like Mary Poppins, a new teacher. Alternatively, groups of children can work together, with your help, to compose a letter to parents asking them to donate items for a school event, e.g. the summer fayre, a jumble sale, a thematic display, sports day.

Starting point

This sheet offers a novel opportunity for the children to write and send letters to family or friends. 'Imaginative' letters can be written too – to or from a story character, TV personality or alien.

Other writing ideas

A letter home from a strange land provides an exercise in descriptive reportive writing; or the children could write a thank-you letter (e.g. to a police officer after a talk about road safety), or a letter of complaint/commendation about a TV or radio programme. Final 'class' versions of the last two can be sent to the appropriate places.

Starting point

Bring in some postcards sent by friends while on holiday. Talk to the children about familiar postcard phrases, e.g. 'Wish you were here.' 'Weather great.' 'Have been on the beach every day.' Then the children can write their own holiday postcards.

Other writing ideas

Look at and talk about postcards used as reminders, e.g. from the dentist about a check-up. Let the children write their own reminder cards.

Display idea

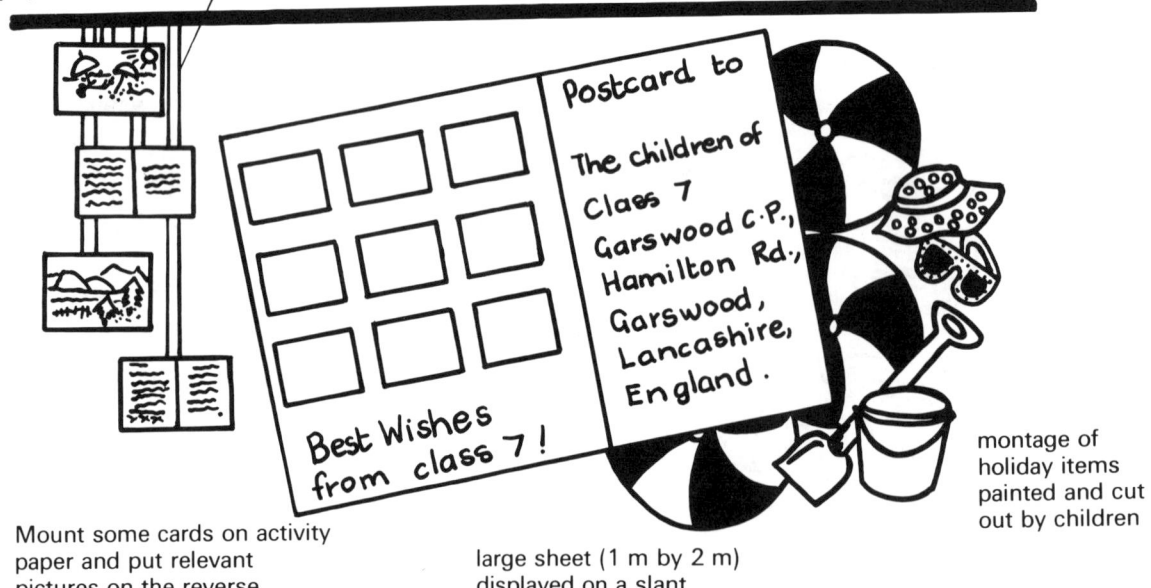

crepe strips 2 cm wide

Postcard to
The children of
Class 7
Garswood C.P.,
Hamilton Rd.,
Garswood,
Lancashire,
England.

Best Wishes
from class 7!

montage of holiday items painted and cut out by children

Mount some cards on activity paper and put relevant pictures on the reverse.

large sheet (1 m by 2 m) displayed on a slant

Starting point

Let the children report school events and make a class newspaper using their own title. They could draw pictures or stick on appropriate photos or cut-out illustrations.

Other writing ideas

Use the sheet as the front page of a newspaper from an imaginary place, e.g. a planet, star or space station; toyland; fairyland; magic woods.

Starting point

Let the children draw a story and add one line of text to each picture. Speech can be added in 'bubbles'.

Other writing ideas

Make a magazine for the class or for an imaginary audience, as suggested for sheet 68, *A newspaper*.

Starting point

Use this sheet to write down a recipe for a school cooking lesson, or for a letter to be sent home requesting ingredients.

Other writing ideas

Find out the school-meal menu and display a carefully written sheet at the entrance to the dining hall. Menu sheets could also be sent to each class.

Write imaginary menus for story characters, e.g. The Three Bears, or for TV/radio series.

Story themes could include *The magic frying pan; A midnight feast; The strange kitchen*.

Starting point

Let the children write spells or warnings in the shape, for use with a hallowe'en story or display, or with fairy stories.

Other writing ideas

This sheet is ideal for a story about a surprise or an explosion. Use it also as a base for verse or descriptive writing about colour, e.g.:

Rolling fire,
Warm, bright, happy,
Startling and surprising.
It makes me jumpy.
Red is my colour.

Display idea

red crepe

red crepe and/or tissue flowers

surprise shape with writing in red pencil or crayon

red or white backing sheets

posters with a predominance of red

red pot

red drape

Once upon a time…
One day…
In a land far away…
Last year…
I must tell you about…
One day I am going to…
It was a dark, dark night…
I've always wanted to…
Not long ago…
A long, long time ago…
One bright sunny morning…
Every night…

...and they all lived happily ever after.
...and that was the end of that.
It had all been a dream.
...and so goodnight to everyone.
They were all as happy as could be.
So they walked off together.
It had ended, at long last.
The end.

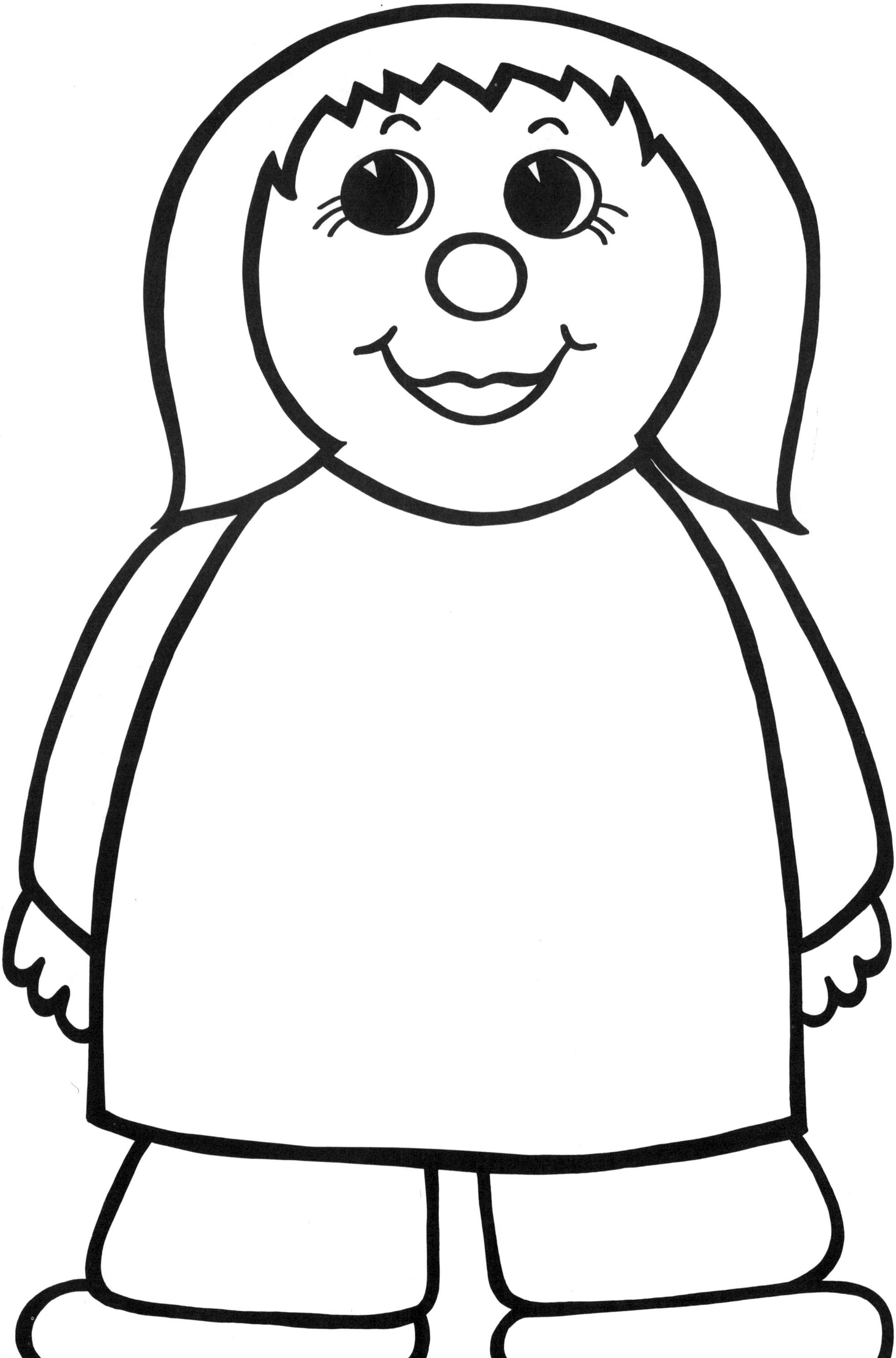

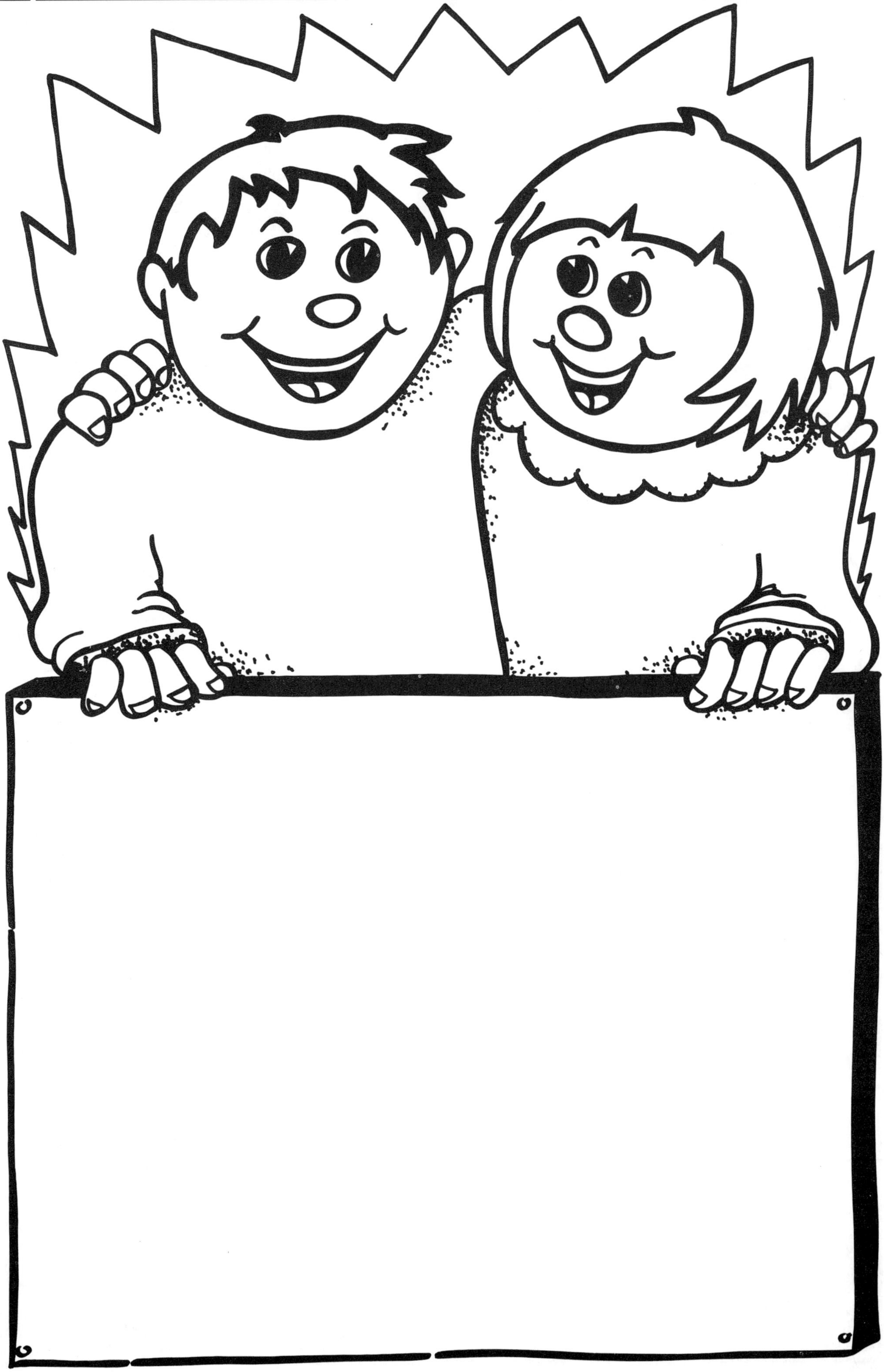

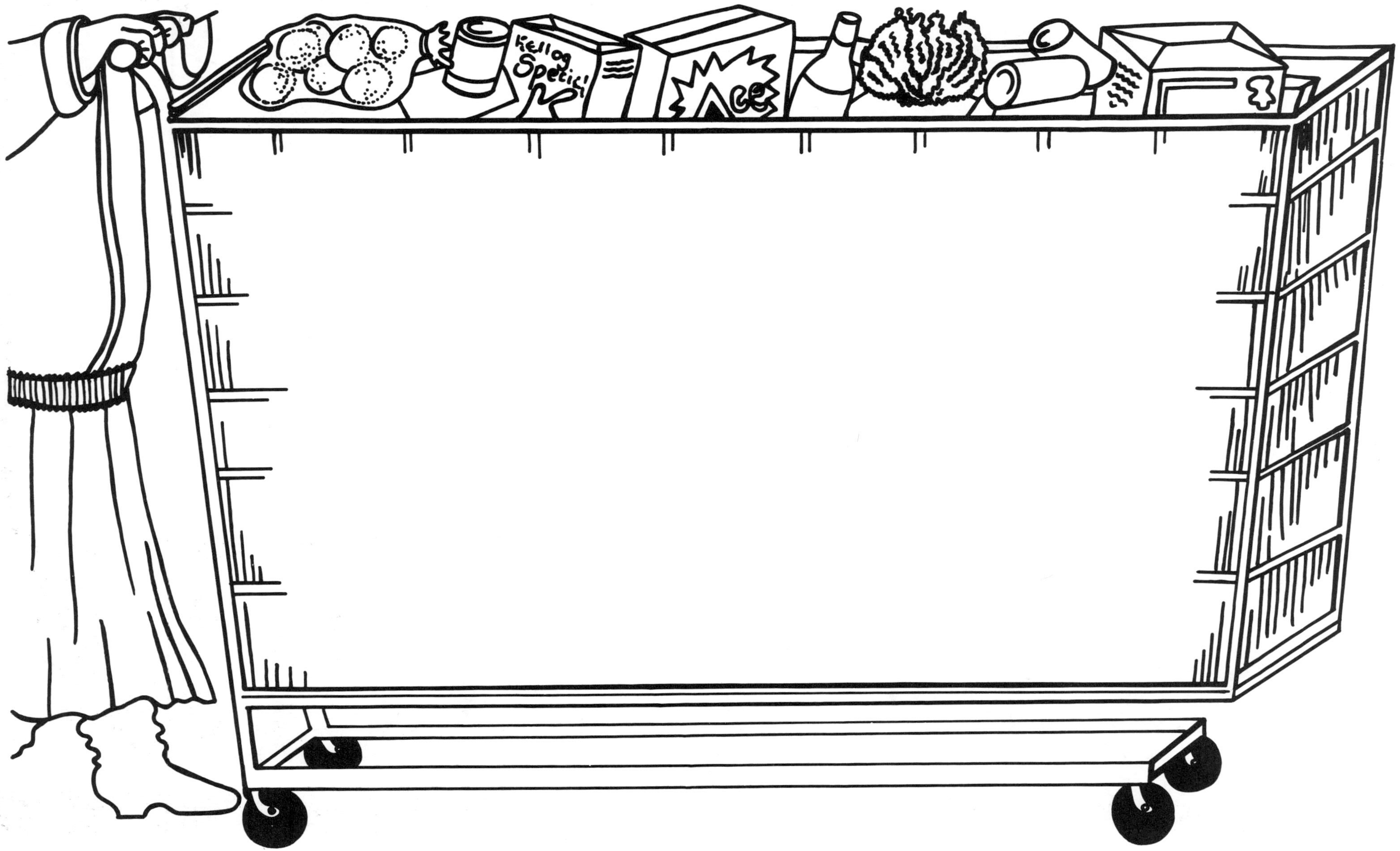
Kellog Spetici
Ace

Out for the day

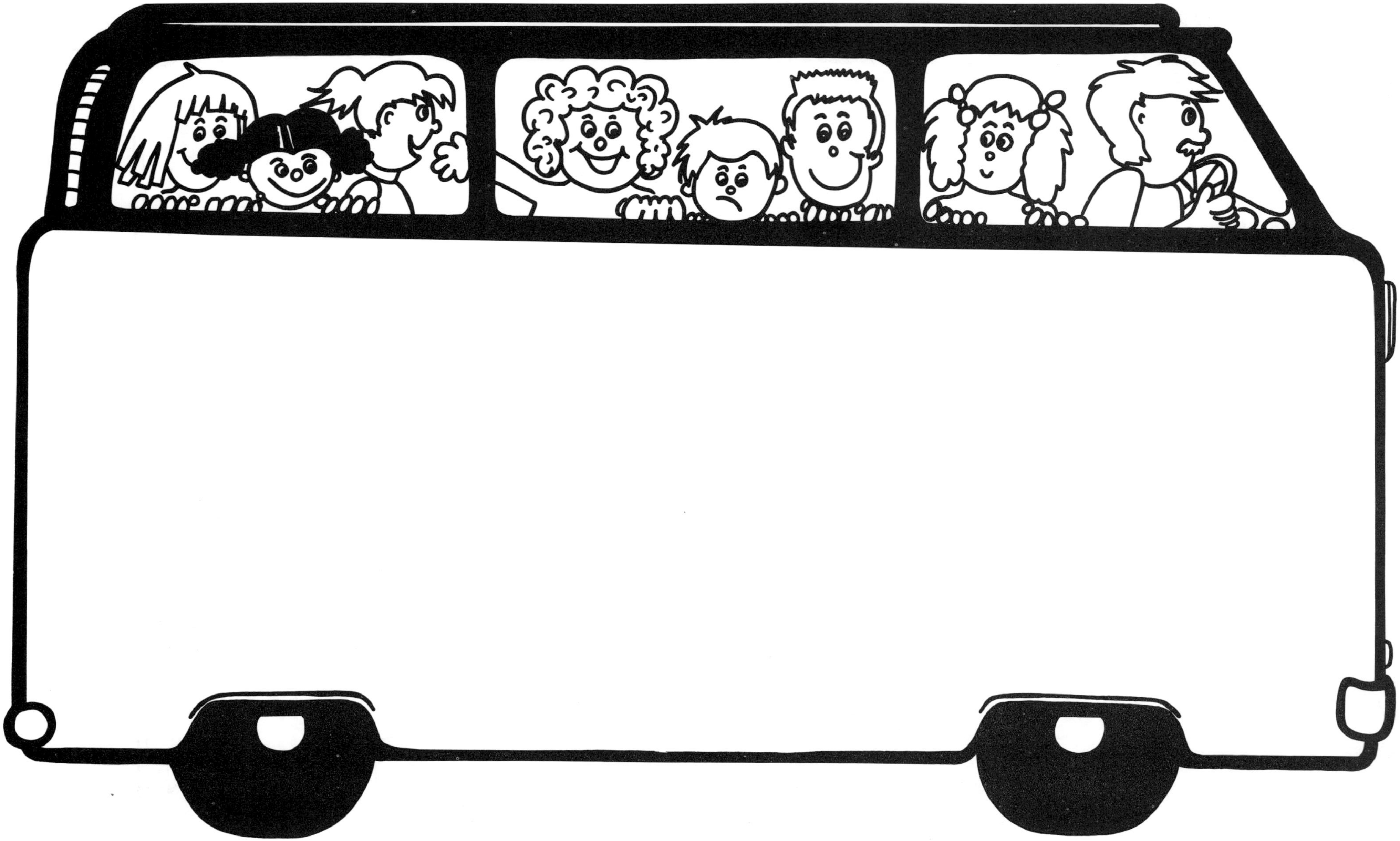

PHILLIPS

Geletex

The hottest day

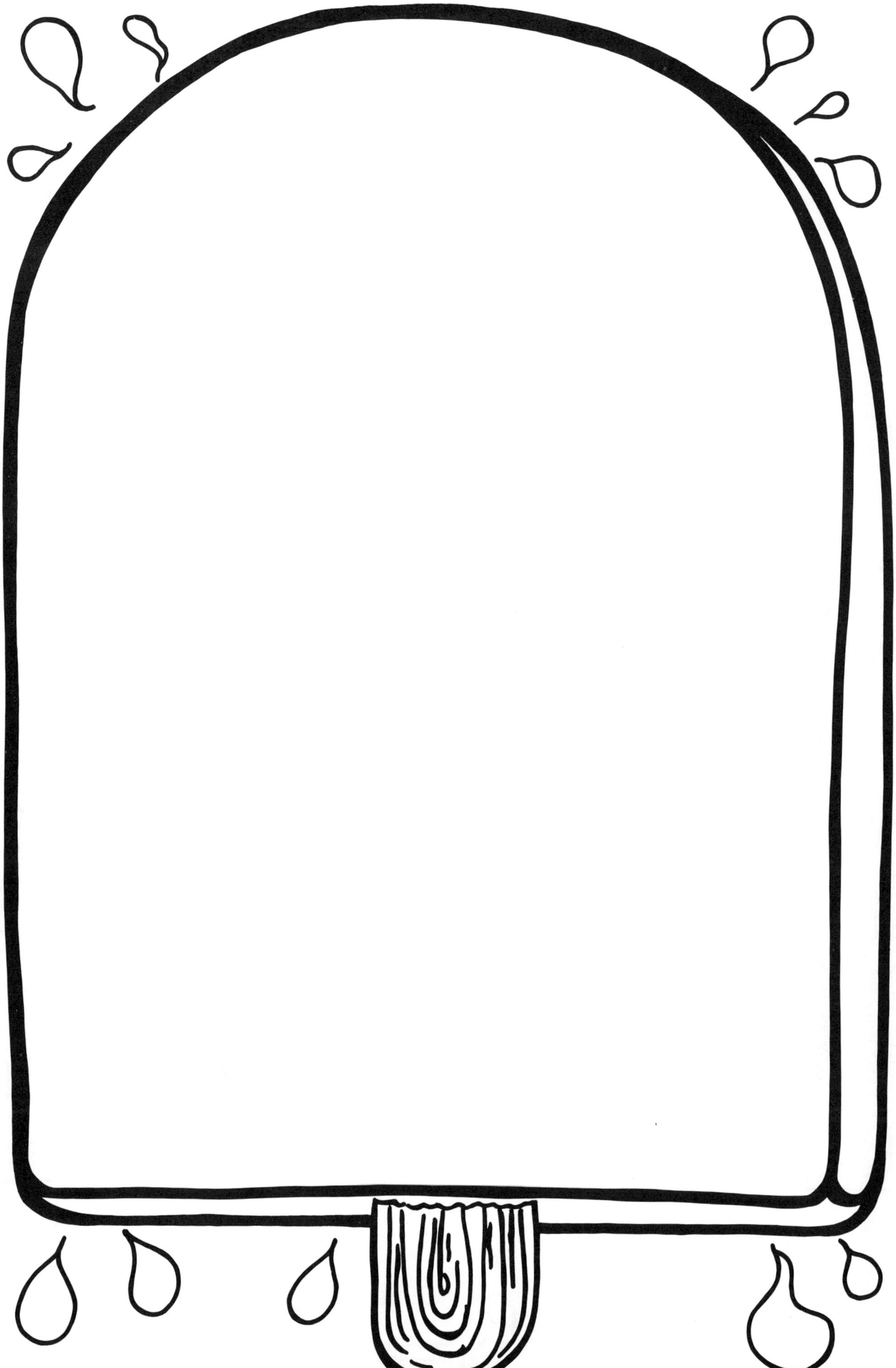

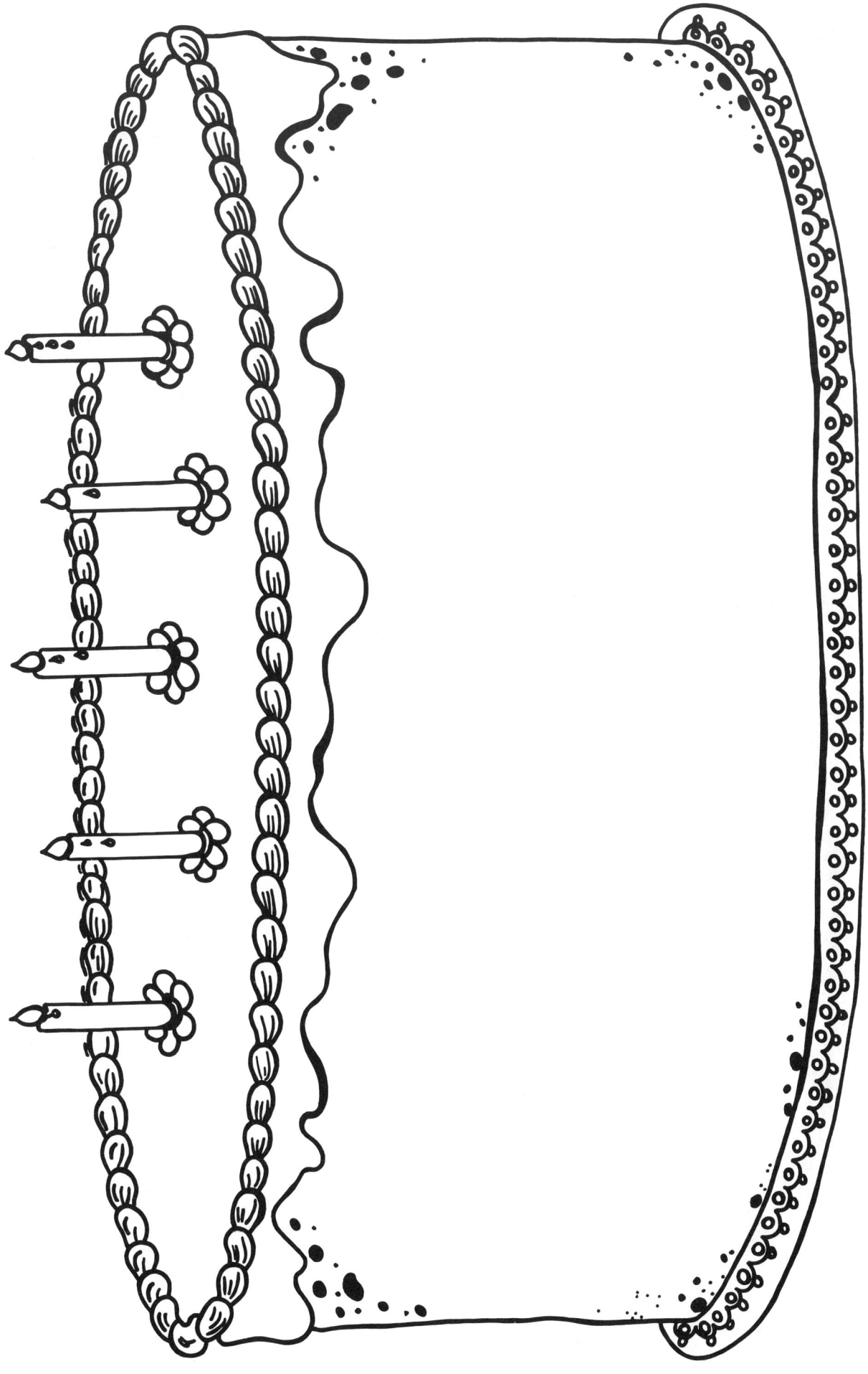

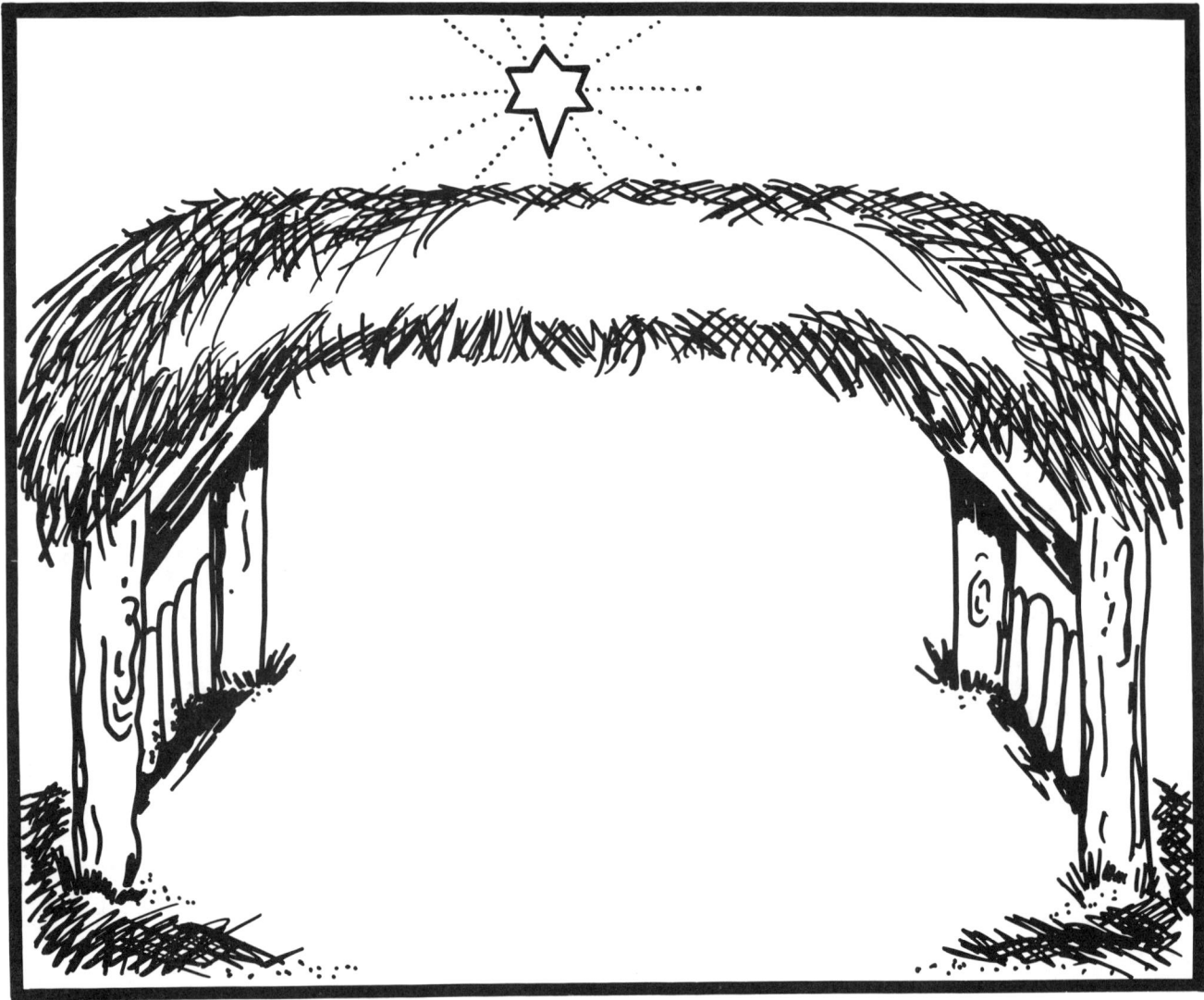

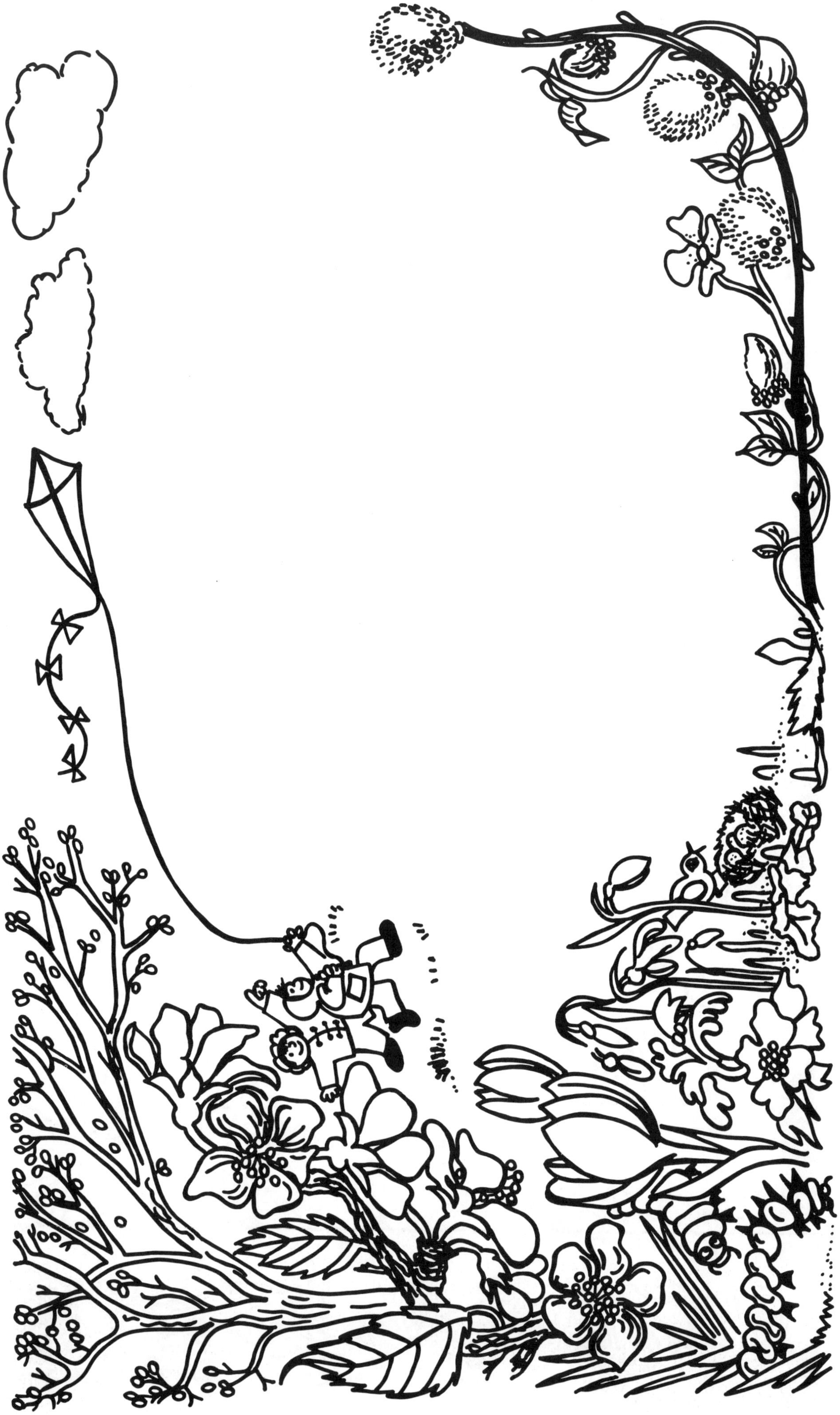

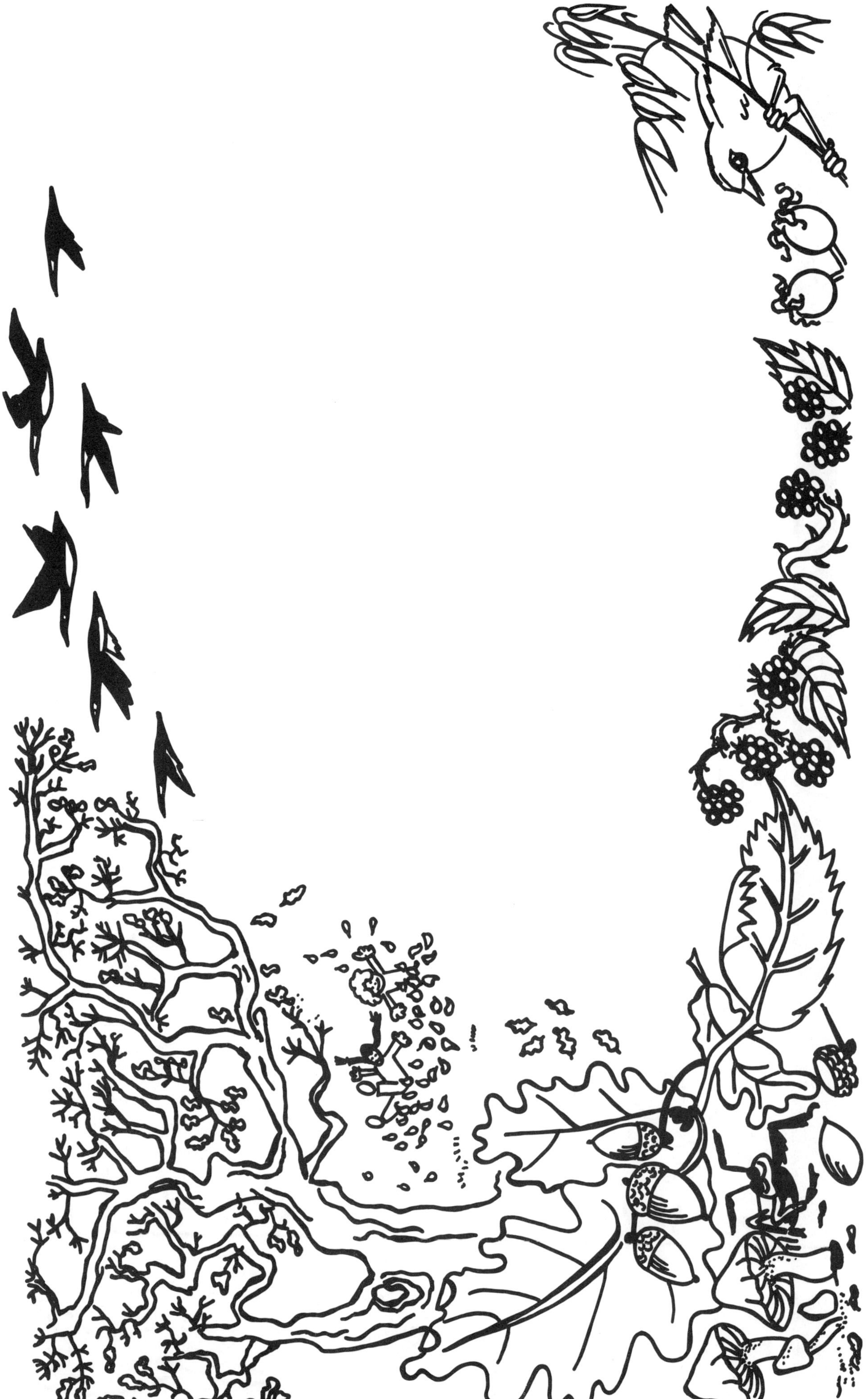

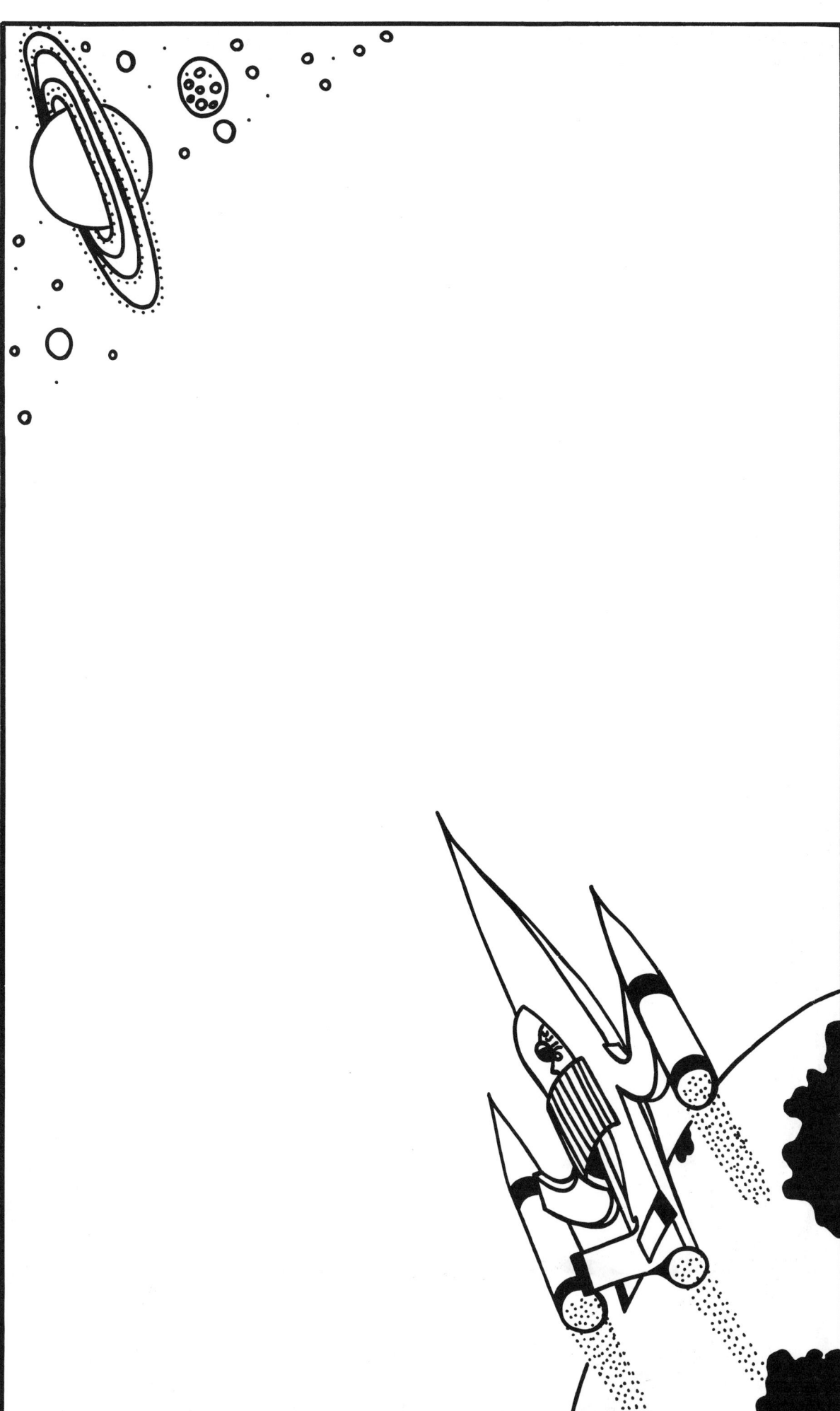

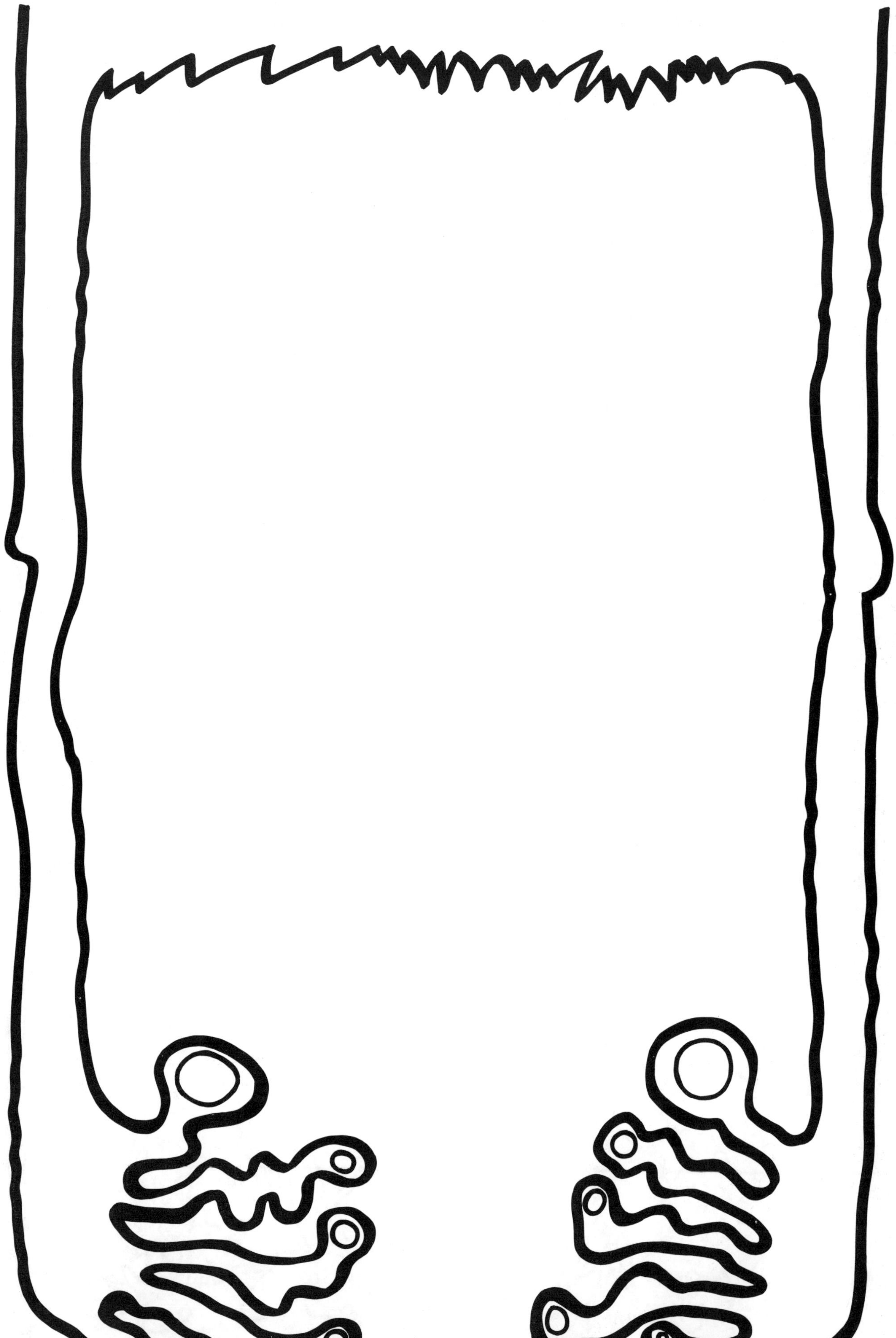

The Daily News

Giant caterpillar

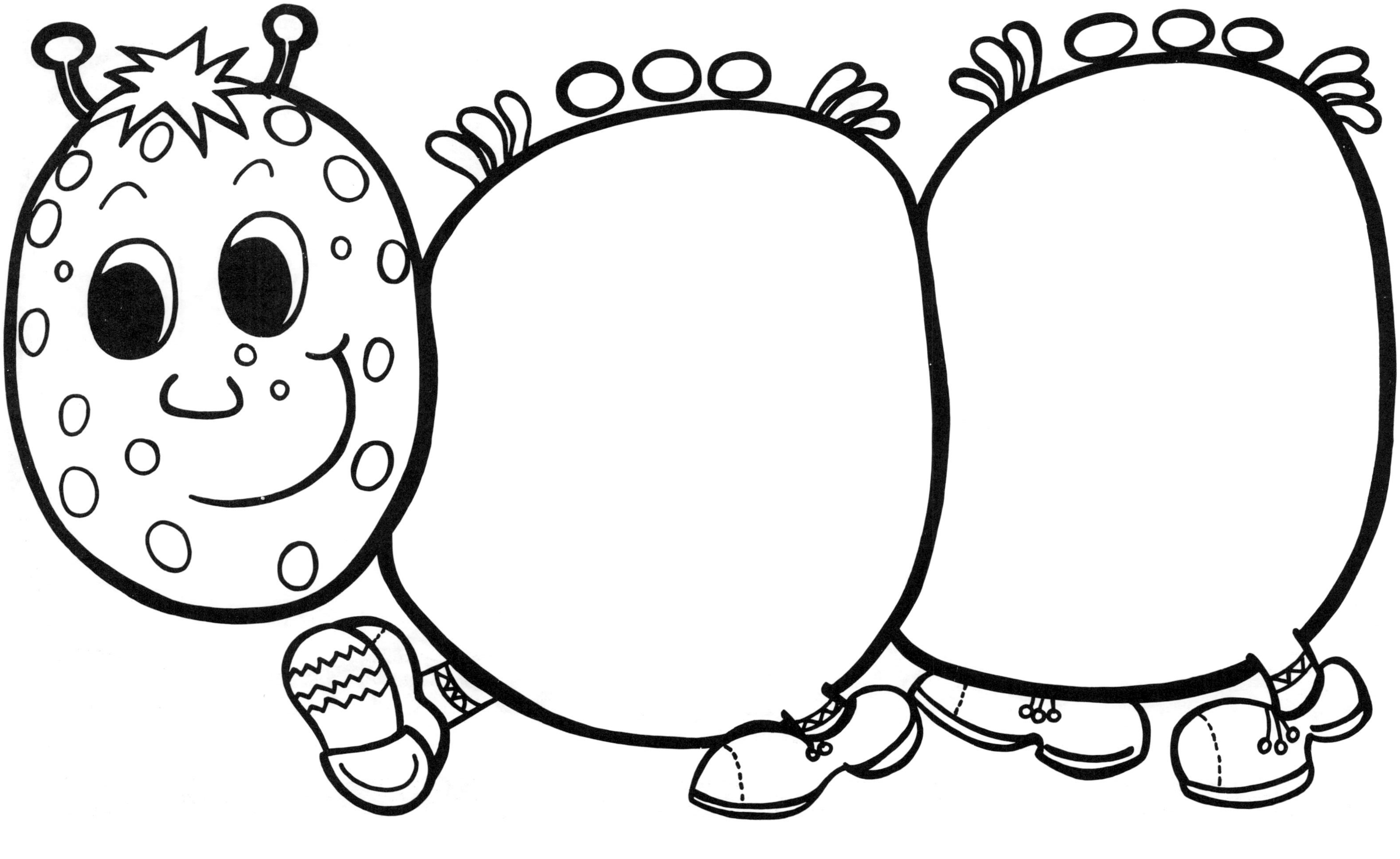

Magic carpet

50

My dragon

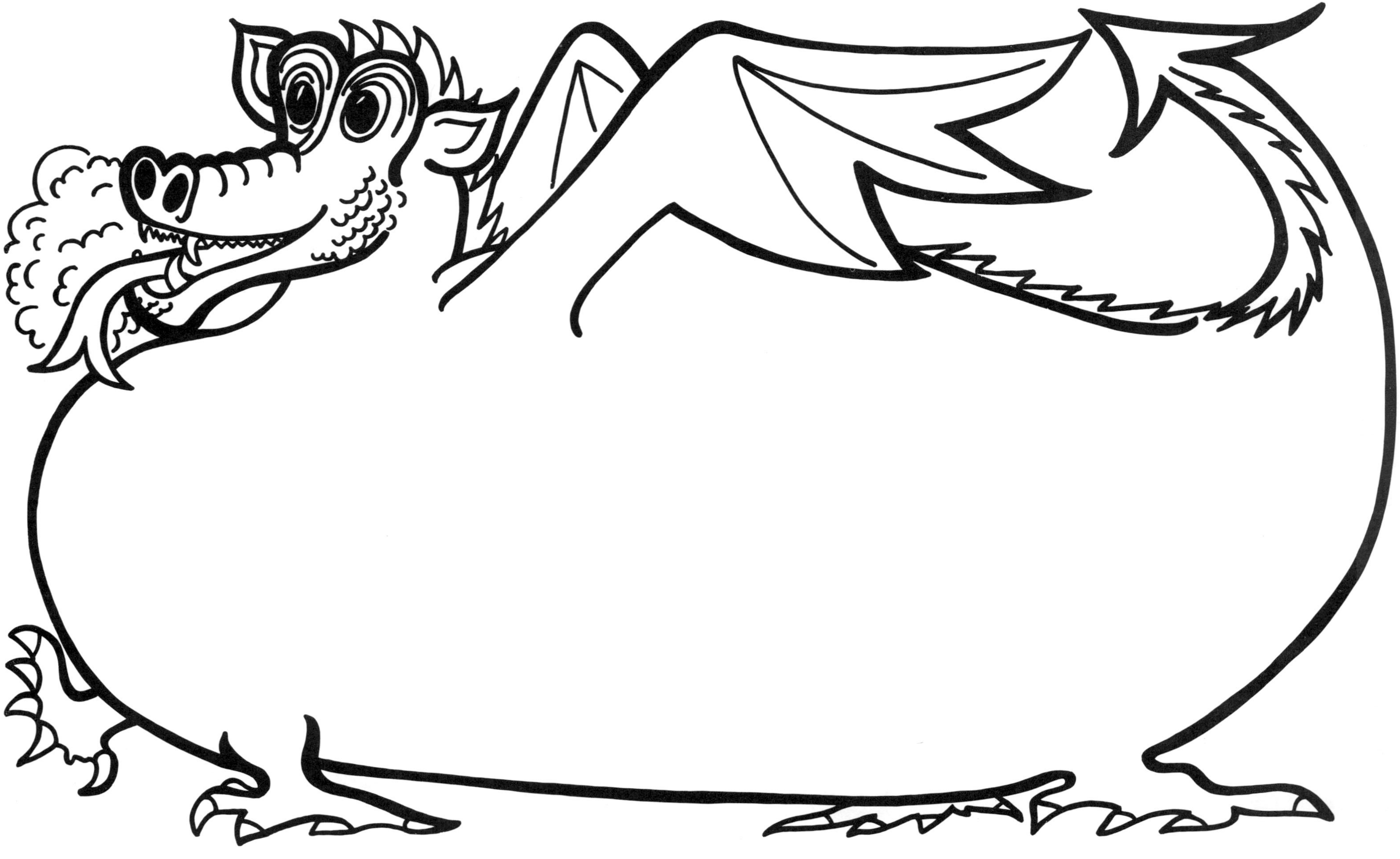

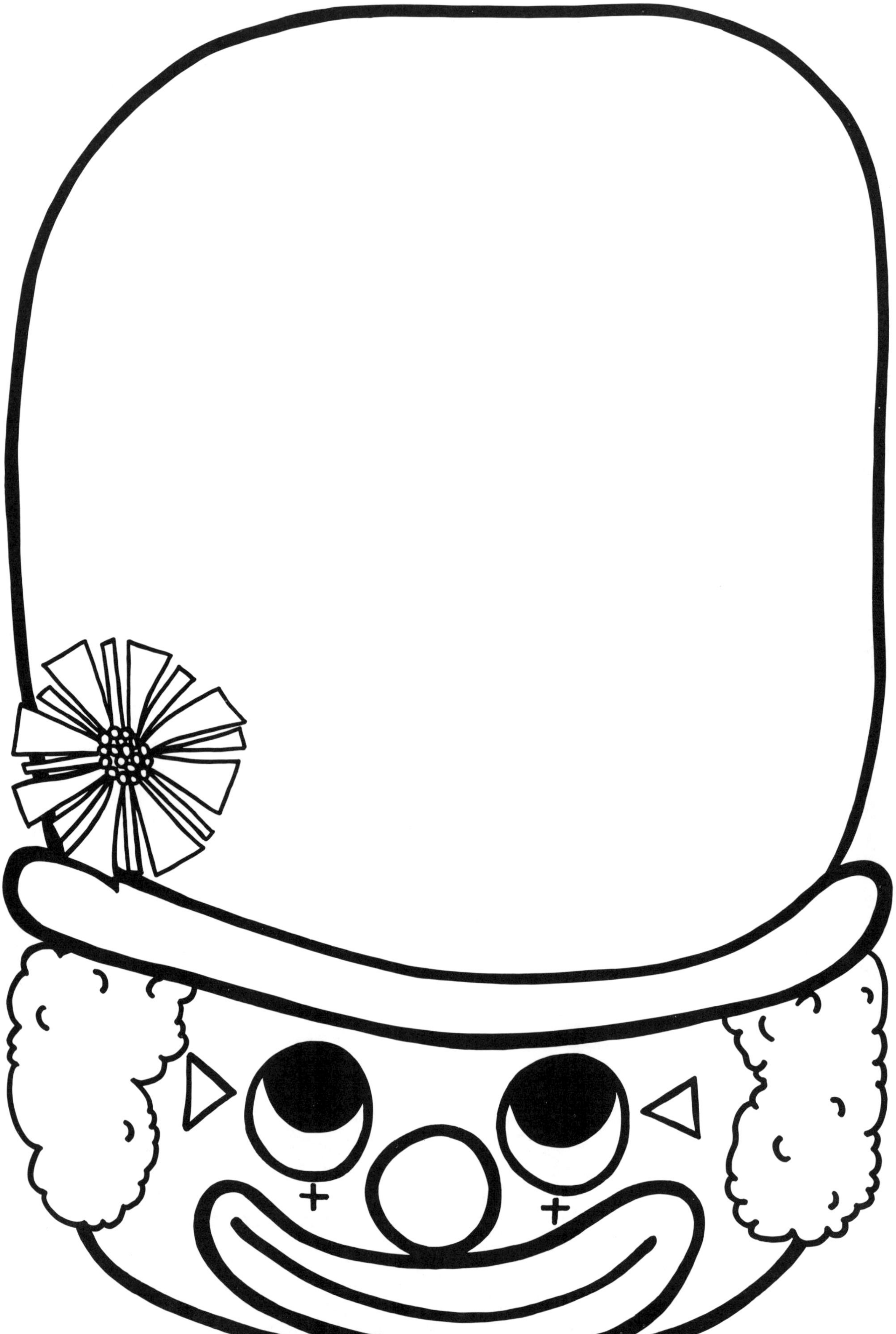

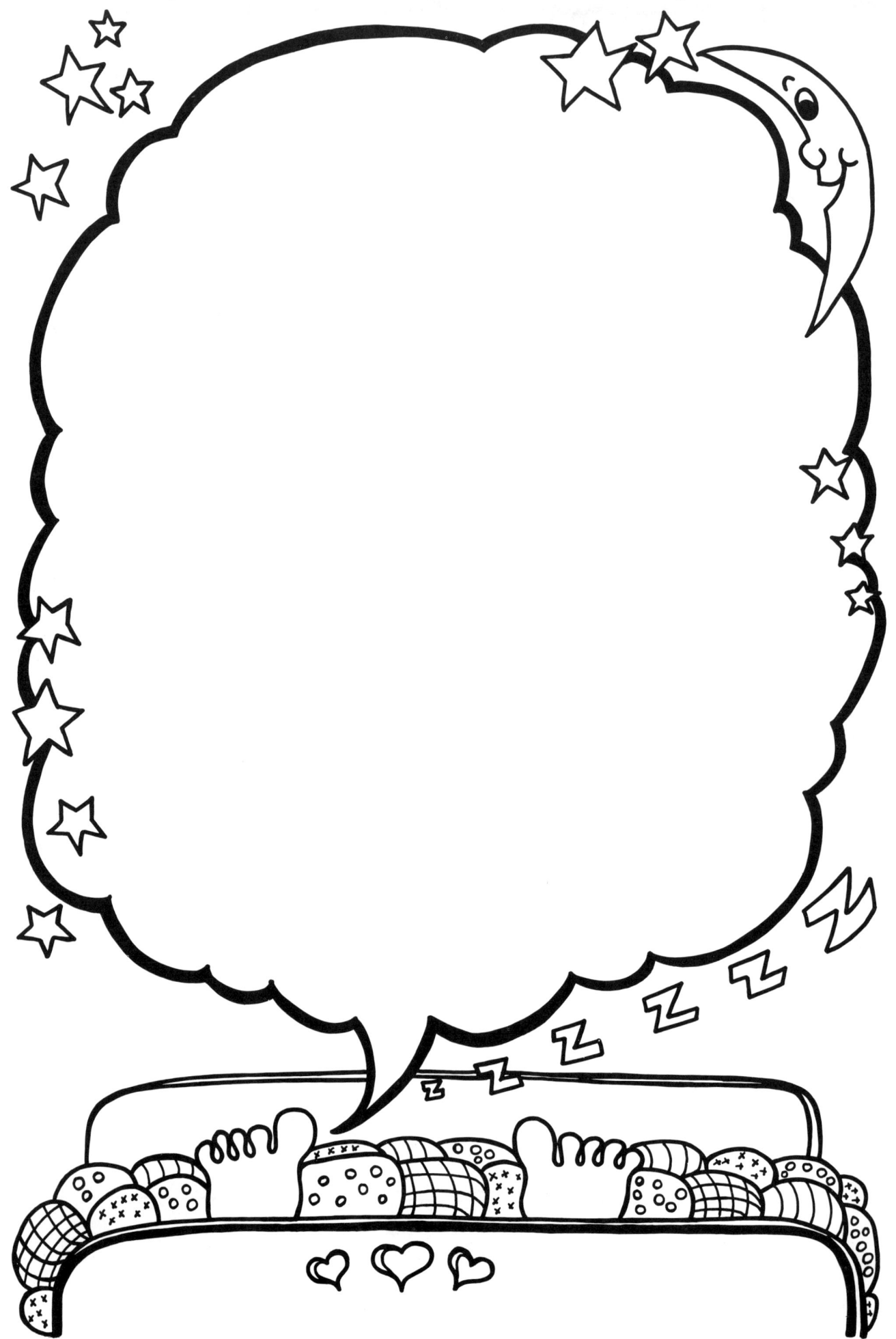

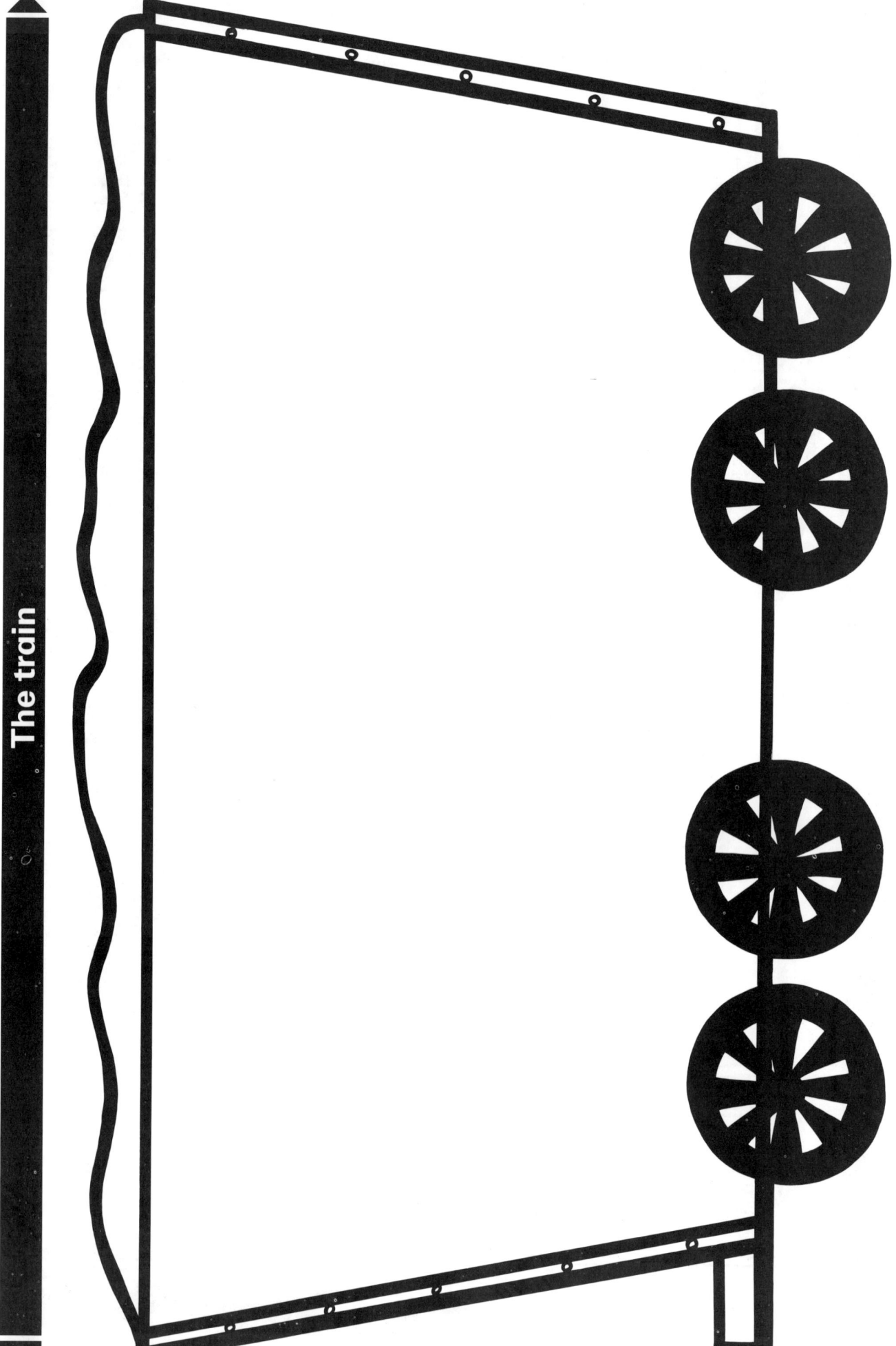

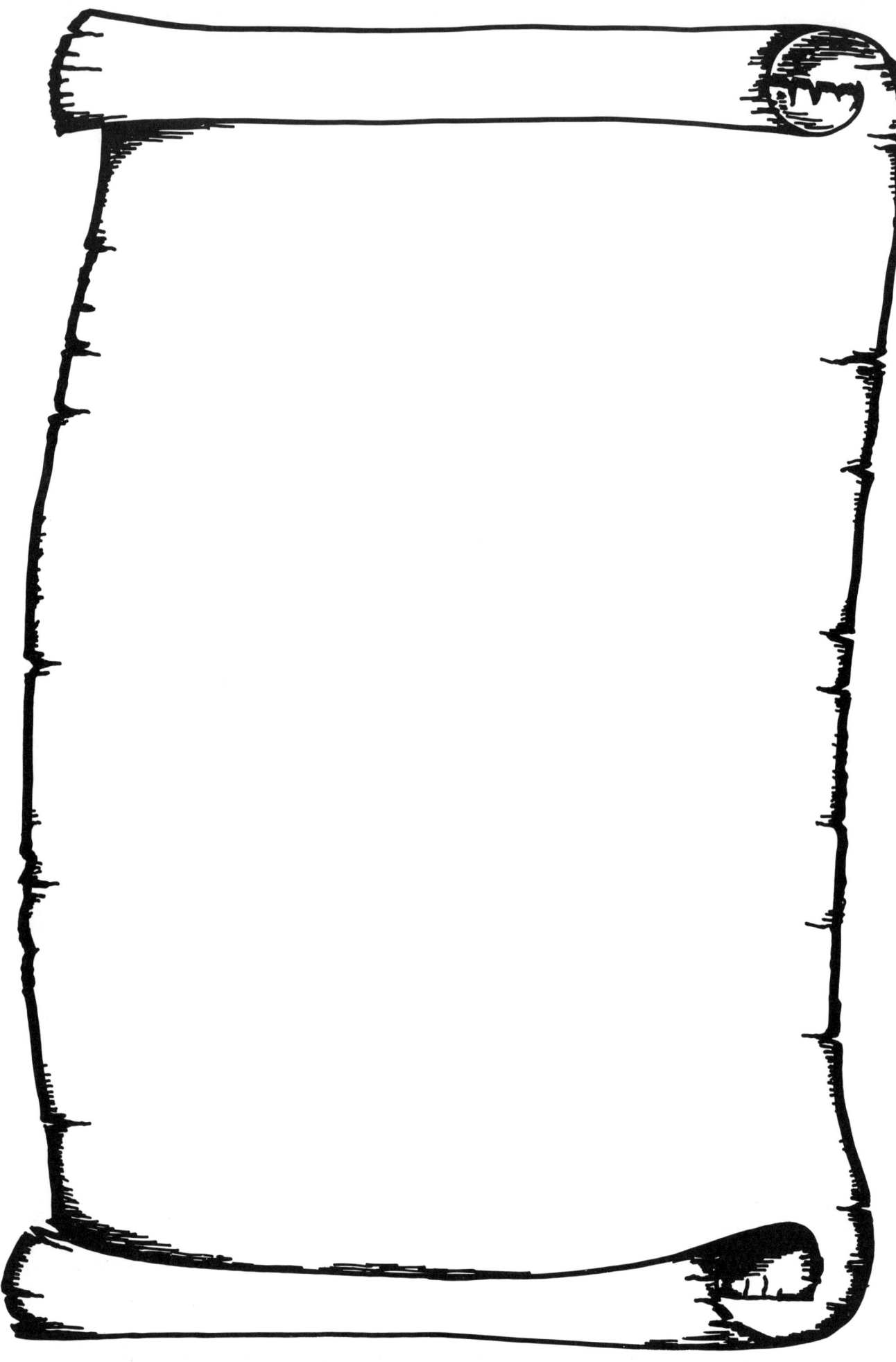

Wanted

for

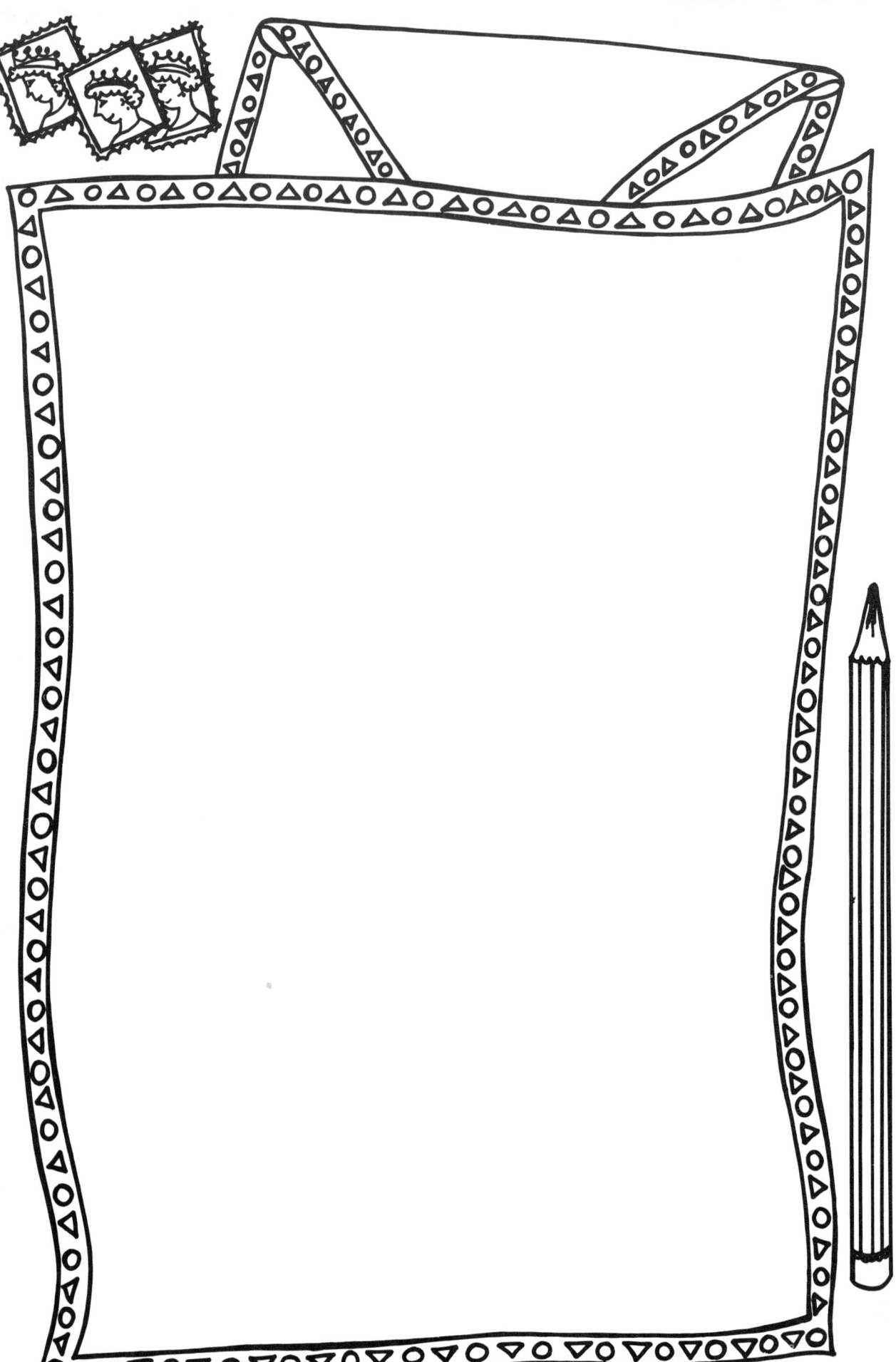

A newspaper

Date	Circulation	Price

Aunt	Aunt	Aunt
Auntie	Auntie	Auntie
baby	baby	baby
brother	brother	brother
cousin	cousin	cousin
Dad	Dad	Dad
Daddy	Daddy	Daddy
Father	Father	Father
Grandad	Grandad	Grandad
Grandpa	Grandpa	Grandpa
Grandma	Grandma	Grandma
Granny	Granny	Granny
Mother	Mother	Mother
Mum	Mum	Mum
Mummy	Mummy	Mummy
sister	sister	sister
Uncle	Uncle	Uncle

Aunt	Aunt	Aunt
Auntie	Auntie	Auntie
baby	baby	baby
brother	brother	brother
cousin	cousin	cousin
Dad	Dad	Dad
Daddy	Daddy	Daddy
Father	Father	Father
Grandad	Grandad	Grandad
Grandpa	Grandpa	Grandpa
Grandma	Grandma	Grandma
Granny	Granny	Granny
Mother	Mother	Mother
Mum	Mum	Mum
Mummy	Mummy	Mummy
sister	sister	sister
Uncle	Uncle	Uncle

assembly	assembly	assembly
book	book	book
Caretaker	Caretaker	Caretaker
chair	chair	chair
child	child	child
children	children	children
classroom	classroom	classroom
Cleaner	Cleaner	Cleaner
Cook	Cook	Cook
corridor	corridor	corridor
desk	desk	desk
Dinner-lady	Dinner-lady	Dinner-lady
friend	friend	friend
hall	hall	hall
Headteacher	Headteacher	Headteacher
home-time	home-time	home-time
number	number	number
Nursery nurse	Nursery nurse	Nursery nurse
paints	paints	paints
paper	paper	paper
pencil	pencil	pencil
playground	playground	playground
playtime	playtime	playtime
pupil	pupil	pupil
reading	reading	reading
Secretary	Secretary	Secretary
table	table	table
teacher	teacher	teacher
Welfare lady	Welfare lady	Welfare lady
writing	writing	writing

The Christmas story – vocabulary

afraid
Angel Gabriel
angel host
Baby Jesus
Bethlehem
born
cattle
census
desert
donkey
frankincense
gifts
gold
hay
hillside
inn
inn-keeper
Joseph
King Herod
Kings
manger
Mary
myrrh
Nazareth
Romans
sheep
shepherds
stable
star
taxes
travel
Wise Men

Christmastime – vocabulary

balloons	balloons	balloons
bauble	bauble	bauble
card	card	card
carol singing	carol singing	carol singing
chimney	chimney	chimney
church	church	church
decorations	decorations	decorations
dinner	dinner	dinner
fairy	fairy	fairy
Father Christmas	Father Christmas	Father Christmas
games	games	games
holly	holly	holly
ivy	ivy	ivy
message	message	message
mince-pie	mince-pie	mince-pie
mistletoe	mistletoe	mistletoe
night	night	night
party	party	party
plum pudding	plum pudding	plum pudding
presents	presents	presents
Queen	Queen	Queen
reindeer	reindeer	reindeer
ribbon	ribbon	ribbon
Santa Claus	Santa Claus	Santa Claus
sleigh	sleigh	sleigh
snow	snow	snow
star	star	star
stocking	stocking	stocking
tinsel	tinsel	tinsel
tradition	tradition	tradition
tree	tree	tree
turkey	turkey	turkey
wrapping	wrapping	wrapping

Spring – vocabulary

babies
born
buds
chick
cleaning
crocus
daffodil
duckling
eggs
farm
frog spawn
grow
lamb
leaves
longer days
nest
new life
rain
shoot
snowdrop
tulip
warmer
weather
wind
woodland

babies
born
buds
chick
cleaning
crocus
daffodil
duckling
eggs
farm
frog spawn
grow
lamb
leaves
longer days
nest
new life
rain
shoot
snowdrop
tulip
warmer
weather
wind
woodland

babies
born
buds
chick
cleaning
crocus
daffodil
duckling
eggs
farm
frog spawn
grow
lamb
leaves
longer days
nest
new life
rain
shoot
snowdrop
tulip
warmer
weather
wind
woodland

bees	bees	bees
bloom	bloom	bloom
butterflies	butterflies	butterflies
cool	cool	cool
drinks	drinks	drinks
drought	drought	drought
dry	dry	dry
flowers	flowers	flowers
gardening	gardening	gardening
glasses	glasses	glasses
heat	heat	heat
heatwave	heatwave	heatwave
hot	hot	hot
insects	insects	insects
lilo	lilo	lilo
paddling pool	paddling pool	paddling pool
sun	sun	sun
sunbathe	sunbathe	sunbathe
sunburn	sunburn	sunburn
sunhat	sunhat	sunhat
sunshine	sunshine	sunshine
suntan lotion	suntan lotion	suntan lotion
sweat	sweat	sweat
swimsuit	swimsuit	swimsuit
trips	trips	trips
trunks	trunks	trunks
visits	visits	visits

Autumn – vocabulary

berries
brown
change
cold
cooler weather
crisp
crunch
curl
damp
dry
dying
fall
fog
fruit
gold
harvest
heap
kick
leaves
mists
nuts
orange
piles
plenty
rain
rake
red
russet
shorter days
spiral
tumble
tumbling
twist
vegetables
winds

berries
brown
change
cold
cooler weather
crisp
crunch
curl
damp
dry
dying
fall
fog
fruit
gold
harvest
heap
kick
leaves
mists
nuts
orange
piles
plenty
rain
rake
red
russet
shorter days
spiral
tumble
tumbling
twist
vegetables
winds

berries
brown
change
cold
cooler weather
crisp
crunch
curl
damp
dry
dying
fall
fog
fruit
gold
harvest
heap
kick
leaves
mists
nuts
orange
piles
plenty
rain
rake
red
russet
shorter days
spiral
tumble
tumbling
twist
vegetables
winds

Winter – vocabulary

balls	balls	balls
blanket	blanket	blanket
books	books	books
chatter	chatter	chatter
clouds	clouds	clouds
cold	cold	cold
crystal	crystal	crystal
drifts	drifts	drifts
fall	fall	fall
flakes	flakes	flakes
freezing	freezing	freezing
frost	frost	frost
frozen	frozen	frozen
gloves	gloves	gloves
hail	hail	hail
ice	ice	ice
icicles	icicles	icicles
rain	rain	rain
scarf	scarf	scarf
scarves	scarves	scarves
shake	shake	shake
sheet	sheet	sheet
shiver	shiver	shiver
sleet	sleet	sleet
sleigh	sleigh	sleigh
slide	slide	slide
slip	slip	slip
snow	snow	snow
snowman	snowman	snowman
splat	splat	splat
throw	throw	throw
toboggan	toboggan	toboggan
wellies	wellies	wellies
wind	wind	wind